CATHARINA COENEN

UNEXPLODED ORDNANCE

What she felt. What they feared.
How they survived. What they saw.

ESSAYS

RESTLESS BOOKS
NEW YORK • AMHERST

First Restless Books paperback edition October 2025

Paperback ISBN: 9781632064059
Library of Congress Control Number: 2025940434

Quotations from "Good Bones" by Maggie Smith, first published in *Waxwing*, 2016, reprinted by permission of the author. Quotations from *The Dream of a Common Language* and *A Wild Patience Has Taken Me This Far* by Adrienne Rich reprinted by permission of W. W. Norton.

This book is supported in part by an award from the National Endowment for the Arts.

Cover design by Beth Steidle
Text design and typesetting by Tetragon, London
Cover illustrations of girls by iStock/Martin Barraud; textured mat, *Stijfselverfpapier in groen met ingedrukt bloemmotief*, courtesy of Rijksmuseum; gift of F. G. Waller, Amsterdam.

Printed in the United States

1 3 5 7 9 10 8 6 4 2

RESTLESS BOOKS
NEW YORK • AMHERST
www.restlessbooks.org

PRAISE FOR *UNEXPLODED ORDNANCE*

"Coenen, a German-born American botanist, has written an arresting collection of essays on what it means to live with political guilt, social trauma, and the unspoken memories not just of what Germany did in World War II, but of what was done to Germany during the conflict. . . . 'The scientist in me pores over . . . data,' she says. But the writer in her recognizes that sometimes you must come to terms with stories that cannot be pegged into a graph or spreadsheet. A memoir of unbearable honesty about a German woman reckoning with war, family, and forgiveness."

— *KIRKUS REVIEWS*

"In lucid and lyrical prose, Catharina Coenen pieces together fragments of her German family's history, through Hitler's rise to power, WWII, and its aftermath. Writing in the English gives this poet and botanist a new language in which to explore the legacies of a people silenced by trauma and guilt. Coenen focuses on her family, but the narrative expands to include the universal realities of war. She channels her ancestors and witnesses with them the violences they both experienced and participated in, violences that will continue to reverberate through generations until they can be acknowledged and mourned. A beautiful and tenderly rendered debut."

— CARMEL McMAHON, AUTHOR OF *IN ORDINARY TIME*

"What makes *Unexploded Ordnance* unusual is its range—you'll notice it from the table of contents onward, this rat-tat-tat of memoir, history, biology, philosophy, linguistics. But what makes it so singular, so special, is how these disparate parts come together, come alive. I read it, entranced—it's a book that should be impossible, yet here it is."

— MENACHEM KAISER, AUTHOR OF *PLUNDER: A MEMOIR OF FAMILY PROPERTY AND NAZI TREASURE*

"A triumph in gripping, masterful prose chronicling the lives of three generations of German women marked by war. What do we know when we know our mother's, our grandmother's stories? With each perfectly nuanced essay, *Unexploded Ordnance* reminds us of the silences we must choose to break. A poignant and unforgettable debut!"

— ANI GJIKA, AUTHOR OF *AN UNRULED BODY*

"What happens to the body after trauma? To the bodies of those descended from trauma? What becomes of desire that has been subsumed?

"These are the questions that arise from this staggering collection of essays, one that brilliantly examines the legacy and inheritance of trauma in three generations of German women. The hurts and silences, ambitions and dignities of grandmothers, aunts, mothers, and daughters take center-stage, giving voice to a range of experiences that feel both timely and timeless. As Coenen reflects on how she came to her own queer identity, she does not shrink from examining her family's past, sharing stories that implicate the suffering caused by her grandparents' Nazi ties as a powerful act against secret-keeping.

"*Unexploded Ordnance* invites the reader to think, perhaps for the first time, about the intersection of science, immigration, choice, and memory. Coenen's perspective as a biologist informs how she brings the personal and political together, allowing the reader to see as a scientist, but through an artist's gaze. And yet, beneath the strength of her voice—frank, tender, wise—there is a way in which her expertise disappears into the work itself.

"Coenen also challenges our perception of what nonfiction can be. Her approach shows both an urgency and a formal inventiveness. No two essays feel the same, and yet there is a powerful sense of cohesion in the reading experience, as well as a sense of awe—the essays are themselves small grenades thrown against walls of silence, denial, and shame. If it is the duty of the scientist to explore the natural world, Coenen does it beautifully by turning her focus to our most basic makeup: the stories we carry in our genes. We are all beneficiaries of her courage and determination."

— RESTLESS PRIZE FOR NEW IMMIGRANT WRITING JUDGES GRACE TALUSAN, JIAMING TANG, AND ILAN STAVANS

The time will come when you, too, will speak,
unrestrainedly like a church bell.

ANI GJIKA, *AN UNRULED BODY*

CONTENTS

UNEXPLODED ORDNANCE

Blindgänger, n. m.

Unexploded ordnance. Literally, the word *Blindgänger*, in German, might mean "blind walker." Its first recorded uses date from right after World War I. Maybe the word arose as a way to describe grenades that failed to reach the target at which they were aimed. Maybe it describes how a bomb falling from an aircraft digs a U-shaped path through soil, a blind tunnel below the earth.

Other suggested translations of this word include dud, misfit, or dead loss. But when German newspapers report that a construction crew has found a *Blindgänger*, they don't mean that the backhoe excavator's bucket clunked against a thing that fails to work properly, or a person whose behavior or attitude sets them apart from others in an uncomfortably conspicuous way, or a venture that produces no profit. What they mean is that it's time to evacuate the entire district, including all of the folks in the nursing homes and hospitals who are hooked up to machines. They mean it's time to stop the trains. They mean it is time to bring in the specialists who can defuse a five-hundred-pound, unexploded bomb from World War II. Or, in case the detonator cannot be removed safely, that it is time to also evacuate everyone adjacent to the transportation route, along which intrepid workers will operate machines to gently—oh-so-gently—ferry the *Blindgänger* to a place where it can be detonated. Or they might be referring to bombs too dangerous to lift or touch: that it is time to explode the dud right there and to rebuild whatever it destroys.

In Berlin alone 7,300 *Blindgänger* have been removed in one of these three ways since 1947. The city government assumes that there are likely 3,000 more. *Blindgänger* are part of life in Germany, part of the cost of doing excavations, part of plowing any field.

The proto Indo-European root of "blind," *bhel-, means to shine, flash, or burn. Who here is blinded by a burn or flash? The pilot? The bomb? The war? Or the construction worker pulling levers on the backhoe? The farmer plowing his field? Or is it the child stumbling through a house, a country where explosions and silence happen inexplicably, the child who learns to tiptoe, who can't tell you why exactly she feels so afraid?

INHERITANCE

1

Maybe it was the smell of slowing trains that drove my heartbeat into my throat. The heating brakes, perhaps, the screams of steel-rimmed wheels, or the decelerating strobe of shadows cast by electric poles. I knew no word to describe the sudden narrowing and darkening of the world, the sweaty hands, the single-minded focus on having to catch my connection, the sense that anything—anything!—would be better than having to wait on a platform or inside a station hall, even in pleasant weather, even with a novel, even for an hour or less. At twenty, when I rode three connecting trains back and forth across northern Germany from college to home two or three times every week, I would have simply named the feeling "changing trains." Doctors, had I thought to consult them, would have labeled it "panic attack." They would have deemed the cause "unknown."

2

In humans, just like in many other mammals, fear can be measured by the extent of a startle response: how forcefully we twitch or jump when we are exposed to a sudden loud noise. When researchers waft acetophenone, a volatile molecule whose receptors in the nose are well-characterized, through the cages of young mice and then apply electroshocks, these mice, now trained to fear the scent of acetophenone, will startle more violently in response to sudden noise than they would without the scent. When the grandchildren of these mice smell acetophenone, they will also startle more violently, even though they were never shocked themselves. The scientists at Emory University who discovered this in 2013 can't tell us whether these fearful mice experience tunnel vision as they twitch. We can't know what thoughts course through mouse brains as muscles jolt. These mice are unaware that the scent of acetophenone also scared their grandparents because this fear response travels from one generation to the next not through learned behavior, observation, or stories told, but in the form of chemical marks that cling to strands of DNA.

3

My mother blamed my post-train exhaustion, my silence, and my fuzzy-mindedness on the lamentable condition of the Deutsche Bundesbahn: the grime, the drafts, the perpetual delays. I knew she avoided train travel at all costs. I thought she was just scared of germs.

4

After nearly a decade in the United States, a country where trains account for less than 0.6 percent of total passenger miles, I returned to Germany to discover that not everybody dreaded trains. Friends used the word "relaxing." They talked about reading, about daydreaming in window seats while nursing cups of tea. It sounded wonderful. I imagined warming to journeying by rail like a child growing into the taste of asparagus. On weekend trips with friends, I gazed at geraniums dangling from hanging baskets along tiny Black Forest stations. I smiled at rivers tumbling through gorges, blooming apple trees, half-timbered towns, the multilayered bicycles encrusting every banister, fence, and bike rack around Freiburg's main station hall. But on any solo trip involving a change of trains, my body ignored these charms: relentless, it served up mounting dread, sweat, racing pulse, tunnel vision, and lingering, numb exhaustion.

5

My mother sympathized with my vague complaints. I told her I was fine. I told myself I didn't have to travel alone all that often. I told myself I was okay. After a few years, I moved back to America, where my Pennsylvanian Rust Belt town had seen its last passenger train twentysomething years before I arrived. I stopped thinking about trains. After another decade or so, they also stopped appearing in my dreams.

6

DNA is a cargo train running from past to future. Meiosis, the cell division that makes sperm or egg, is a shunting yard, where 23 chromosomes assemble into new configurations like freight cars: yes, Dad's blue eyes—no, Mom's green; yes, Mom's long arms—no, Dad's calm. It's Gregor Mendel's lottery, played out with vast information stores, according to rules he first described, as it happens, during the initial heyday of public railroads, in 1865. Mendel knew nothing about chromosomes or DNA, and yet, after growing 28,000 pea plants in the garden at St. Thomas Abbey, he could see how some pieces of information traveled across generations together, like fellow passengers in a single carriage, whereas other pieces frequently parted company as genomes passed through the switchyard between one generation and the next. We've only recently discovered other rules, the "epigenetics" superimposed on Mendel's genetic laws: how methyl marks can lock some DNA away for a generation or two or three. In mice, the genes locked down by trauma contain the code for play, exuberance, unencumbered joy.

7

A few months after Mendel first told the Natural History Society of Brno, Moravia, about inheritance in peas, a train carrying passengers from the English Channel ferries at Folkestone Harbour toward London slid from a viaduct. The crash, at forty miles per hour, killed ten passengers, injured forty more, and dumped Charles Dickens into a muddy riverbed. Dickens staggered among the corpses, drizzled brandy from his hip flask between the lips of the injured, then crawled back into his broken car and pulled manuscript pages—the most recent installment of *Our Mutual Friend*—from the muck. Though physically uninjured, he could not speak for two weeks. During the five remaining years of his life, he avoided rail travel at nearly any cost. Dickens was far from alone in his dread of trains: Two years after the accident, the British physician John Eric Erichsen coined the diagnosis "railway spine" for sufferers of nightmares, sleep disturbances, and memory gaps after railroad disasters and other traumatic events.

8

"They are climbing the fences," my mother explains over the phone when I ask why she can't sleep at night, "just trying to get into the Chunnel to England." When the rail tunnel under the English Channel opened in 1994, eliminating the slow and uncomfortable ferry crossing for journeys between mainland Europe and the British Isles, the idea of traveling for nearly thirty miles under 250 feet of water struck me as suffocating, impossible, even if—or maybe because—at 100 miles per hour, the Chunnel trains pop back into light and air within fifteen minutes of plunging underground. Now, twenty years later, I must wonder: How much desperation does it take for human beings to *want* to walk thirty miles, most of it under the sea, knowing an oncoming train could kill them at any moment? Throughout the summer and fall of 2015, people tried it by the hundreds or thousands, night after night, despite taller and taller fences built around the Chunnel entrance, infrared monitors, and police. The Chunnel stories raise and shake my mother's voice; it quivers and quakes across the line in modulations I also hear when she talks about children in Aleppo, Damascus, Afghanistan, children slipping from rubber rafts into the Mediterranean Sea. She usually flees the room when news or TV shows touch on war or refugees. The newsreel's strobe-light scenes click deep-wired synapses inside her brain, flood her body with a sleep-defying cocktail of glucocorticoids and catecholamines.

9

When I watch *Tagesschau* online, the same news show my mother has seen on her TV in Germany, a cool-eyed German journalist with straight blond hair reports from London that England has taken "more than its share of immigrants, mostly from Eastern European countries," and that "these people" have been welcomed into the labor force. But for right now, she says, the tide of public opinion has turned, and the British happen to not want any more foreigners at this time: "They see it as a problem that should remain continental." In my mind, I watch this "problem" walking from the French refugee camp dubbed "The Jungle" toward Britain, on legs too short to step from one crosstie to the next. "Walking with all those children," my mother says, her voice jumping a familiar octave of despair, "all those tiny, tired children being dragged along those tracks under the sea." Part of my mother's brain is aware she is watching from her living room. Another part is getting ready to take steps too large for size three shoes.

10

Stuttgart, the closest major city to where my parents now live, has a terminus station. Passengers changing trains pull their roller bags around the noses of locomotives lined up in a row—enormous steel Pony Express horses tied up at a saloon, catching hissing breaths between one mad dash and the next. Across from the railheads, shops and cafés line a spacious station hall. There is no need to change platforms via a clammy underpass, no need to lug heavy bags up and down stairs. Since the arrival of the first train in 1846, no part of Stuttgart's railroad station has been underground. I appreciate the convenience every time I drag my overseas luggage from the InterCity Express that brings me here from the Frankfurt airport to the local train that will take me to my parents' little town. But my stair-free ease today means there was no place to shelter from air raids during the war.

11

My mother asks if I want to look at my Opa Alfred's letters from the Russian front before she throws them out. She digs behind stacks of starched table linens for a ziplock bag with gray military-issue envelopes. She gave up trying to decipher her father's handwriting long ago—even her oldest friends, claiming familiarity with Sütterlin, the old cursive script, capitulated to my grandfather's bad penmanship, worsened by cold hands and haste as the German front line advanced, retreated, and collapsed. We huddle on the couch, ponder crossed-out addresses, pore over lowercase *e*'s that look like check marks, *m*'s that look like *u*'s. A few words slot into place: "My dear . . . little . . . chickie?" Really? Chickie? We look at each other, feel the corners of our mouths creep up into our cheeks, then burst out laughing. My mother, remembering her mother, Lotte, as formidable, shakes her head in disbelief: "I never heard him call her *that*." But nothing else makes sense—it must be right. We smirk, and I know we both think of my grandmother's flying curls, her tiny frame, how she could walk beneath my grandfather's outstretched arm without the top of her hair touching him. "My dear little chickie . . . How . . . are . . . you? How are . . . the . . . cattle?" No way! ". . . the . . . children?" Yes. We guess, intuit, hypothesize, backtrack, skip ahead, give up, have coffee, try again. Out of an ocean of mystery marks, islands of meaning rise like fog. Here. And here. Land bridges form. Slow continents take shape. Around the words, my mother's childhood memories condense like breath on a mirror. Sluggishly, in wisps. A snippet caught before she drifts off into an afternoon nap: the sheep her parents kept during the hunger years after the war, putting her forever off drinking milk. Another fragment, sharp and hot, pierces her morning mind before feet find slippers on the bedside rug: bouncing on the bed as Lotte tries desperately to pull clothes onto her, admonishments inaudible over the air-raid sirens, a stinging slap just moments away. And then, late one night, before she drifts to sleep, the trains start rolling in.

12

My mother does not remember the name of the station that materializes in her midnight memory. But date stamps and crossed-out addresses on gray envelopes map out where she went: from the city of Essen in the Ruhr, where she was born, and where my grandparents grew up and lived, close to Krupp's steel factory, one of the most important targets for Churchill's bombs, all the way to small-town Biberach, far down in the south of rural Swabia, far away from industry. There is no direct train. Stuttgart is where you change.

13

My mother's memory flashes an image, a short video, of sitting across from her mother and sister at a round table in a cavernous, crowded station hall—a terminus station café. Amid the people milling all around, a stranger—a soldier—grabs Lotte's shoulder, asks, "Where are you headed, young woman? You have to take the next train out right now, no matter where it goes! The station is getting bombed."

14

Three hundred and fourteen British bombers flew toward Stuttgart on the evening of March 11, 1943. My mother was not quite four years old, my aunt was five. My Oma Lotte was pregnant with their little brother: my uncle. Over the course of two nights during the first week of March, air raids on Essen had rendered 80,000 people homeless—far too many for officials to stamp evacuation forms, let alone organize temporary housing elsewhere. My grandmother had swept up her shattered dishes and windowpanes, packed two suitcases, and was traveling south, with no idea where she and her two small children would stay. Somewhere rural. Somewhere away from bombs. Even if you don't know where to go, Stuttgart is where you change.

15

The train platform in my mother's memory is so full of people that there is no place to stand, the train overflowing, people hanging from the doors, no hope at all of getting on. But then a soldier grabs her, lifts her up and through a window, pushes her sister in after her as the train lurches, shudders, moves. She screams, her body using every muscle, turning every last molecule of oxygen to sound, as the train begins to roll, rolls toward an unknown destination, rolls away from her mother on the platform, away from the only face she knows. At the last second, two soldiers, running alongside, shove her mother and two suitcases in after the shrieking girl.

16

Three hundred thousand German children were reported missing by the end of World War II. In the madness of trains derailed or rerouted after bomb attacks, the chances of a mother finding two little girls were nil. Missing children posters hung in German railroad stations until late into the 1950s.

Six thousand of these children were still searching for their families thirty years after the war; 400 searches were still registered as "open" at the end of May 2018. Some were lost refugees or evacuees. Some were abducted from Eastern European countries by Nazis for the purpose of "Germanization." Some were Jewish children, hidden away by neighbors or strangers. Some could not yet speak when they were separated from their parents. Many were too young to remember their mother tongue, let alone cities, addresses, names.

17

Unpredictable separation of mouse pups from their mothers rewires their nervous systems. Just like mice trained to fear the scent of acetophenone, the children and grandchildren of these pups inherit both the behavioral hallmarks of depression and the changed structure of the brain.

18

Where did it go, my mother's railroad station terror, the mouse equivalent of acetophenone-scent electroshock? Did it come to me in methyl marks across my DNA? Or did I drink it in through story snippets, told by my grandmother when I was a child, without ever connecting what I had heard then to my adult sweaty palms and racing heart? "You've inherited your father's body type but your mother's nervous system," our family physician used to say, when I would mention clammy hands, darkness nesting in my heart for days on end. Can memories, fragments of experience, or patterns of excitatory synapses—short circuits connecting "hot metal smell in" to "panic out"—travel from one generation to the next? And can I remove them, scrape methyls from the backbone of my DNA, unhook the neurons, undo whatever connection there may be?

19

In 2016, researchers in Zurich, Switzerland, showed that male mice who as pups were separated in unpredictable ways from their mothers are not only incapable of coping with stress as adults, but they also pass on this stress intolerance to their sons. But, if these traumatized mouse pups are raised together with their families in comfy multiroom apartments, complete with the mouse equivalent of a fitness studio and entertainment suite, they turn into adults with normal stress responsiveness, who father sons with normal mouse behaviors in response to stress.

20

To process trauma, humans require more than postwar affluence, more than an easy life among friends and loved ones. Our storytelling brains need hours, days, or years of huddling on the couch, coffee, letters, words to sort now from then, impose a grammar upon neurotransmitter release, fine-tune synaptic networks to gut-feel the difference between past and present tense.

21

Once my mother started talking and remembering, she also began to sit all the way through the news on *Tagesschau* most nights. "I can't believe he's doing this," she said over the phone, seven years ago, referring to the president of the country in which I live, the first time Americans elected a president who promised to deport eleven million undocumented immigrants. "Taking away those children from their parents is a crime! How can he possibly not know he's messing up their entire lives? How can he not know they won't ever be the same?"

22

The InterCity Express from Frankfurt, already ten minutes behind its scheduled arrival time in Stuttgart, decelerates amid hedgerows and Holstein cows. The city is nowhere in sight. Poplars cast slowing shadows across the faces of passengers, across their hands clasping backpack straps and bags. We listen to squealing brakes, glance at cell phones, look at each other, roll our eyes as the overhead speaker crackles, announces a delay, a necessary wait for an oncoming train to clear our track. I feel the corners of my mouth creep up into my cheeks. The weather is neither cold nor sweltering. There'll be another connecting train from Stuttgart into the high Black Forest within an hour or two after we'll arrive. There will be coffee shops with round tables in the station hall. I'll call my parents, read a book. Stuttgart *was* bombed when my mother *was* two. *She was* nearly orphaned. Between reassurance and deterrence, *I am* changing trains.

23

Peace is a through station, a brief stop between one war and the next. By the end of 2026, Stuttgart's main station will no longer be a terminus; it will be underground. Nineteen miles of tunnels will accelerate connections. But they will offer no protection against the nuclear arms of modern war. The European Reassurance Initiative, in response to Russia's annexation of Crimea, was approved at $850 million by the US Congress in 2014, grew to $6.5 billion by 2019, then shrank to a request of $2.9 billion for 2025. Along the way, *Reassurance* became *Deterrence*. To feel peace, the space between two terrors, you have to touch the present tense: put down a toe, like stepping from a train, plant a foot in the moment, this one, less than a breath, between screeching brakes and the lurching shudder of departure.

***schreiben*, v.**

The German verb *schreiben*, "to write," is most closely related to the English verb *to shrive*, which means to hear a confession or to confess.

The English verb "to write," in turn, is derived from the Proto-Germanic **writan*, which means "to tear," or "to scratch"—likely a reference to sign-making before ink: to carve directions into bark, or stone, or skin.

Schreiben, in German, means to bare your soul.

Writing, in English, is a tearing-into: a wounding, a telling-as-a-scar.

THE PRINTING PRESS

WHEN I WAS SIX OR SEVEN, my Oma Lotte read to me the beginning of a novel she was working on. At that time, we both wrote or sketched our drafts in old appointment books: fat daily planners in cushioned black vinyl covers that sales reps dropped as advertisement gifts at my parents' store. In mine, horses with and without necks, drawn in ballpoint pen, ran across dates and times. In hers, a newly married man returns from work to find his young wife knitting in the garden. She has set a coffee table with porcelain dishes and a home-baked cake. Baby-blue yarn clues him in that she is expecting their first child; she shows him another skein in pink to indicate they will have twins. He rejoices, she blushes, the thought of discussing pregnancy eliciting shared pride and embarrassment.

My grandmother dreamed of becoming a writer all her life. When she was a child, her mother, like many women in the workers' quarters of Essen, Germany, took in lodgers, subletting a room in their apartment, often to single men, in order to supplement the family's income. The man who lived with Lotte's family throughout her childhood appeared in anecdotes she told about her youth as "the Uncle"—an honorific that children in Germany were expected to bestow on family friends. Lotte's parents must have felt great affection for this subletter because they named Lotte's younger brother, Norbert, after him.

Lotte's Uncle Norbert made his living by sewing; a clubfoot kept him from taking on better-paid work in Essen's coal mines or steel factories. When he was born, orthopedic interventions for this common condition, such as the Ponseti method of casting the foot to gradually redirect its growth, were still half a century away. Most children born with a clubfoot, not to mention more profound disabilities, were left with lifelong pain when walking or standing.

Sewing for a living meant that Norbert was nearly always home. His disability also kept him home when other men were sent to the trenches during World War I, which ended when Lotte was barely six years old. I don't know how old she was when Norbert moved in. But as I try to imagine her sitting with Uncle Norbert while he sewed, I draw on my own early memories of my father's father, Konrad: I spent many hours of my first years in a playpen my parents plopped right onto Opa Konrad's workbench in the sewing shop above our store. Later I would often sit on a low wooden stool that the seamstresses in the shop used to climb onto the worktable or to crouch down to pin a customer's hem. I remember the swish-swish of the big tailor's scissors as they cut cloth along lines drawn with sharp-edged squares of waxy tailor's chalk; how the cool smoothness of plastic, metal, and mother-of-pearl hugged my hands as I rifled through deep bins filled with stray buttons, hunting for treasures to string onto sturdy threads, making necklaces. In Lotte's home, just like in mine, tailors, marooned on their workbenches, made for dependable babysitters, chatting with children, telling stories, looking up just in time to say "No, don't put that in your mouth."

Behind bits of conversation and jokes tossed back and forth between seamstresses in my grandfather's tailor shop, behind the hiss of the steam iron, the rat-tat-tat of sewing machines, behind the whoomph of the ventilators that suctioned cloth to the enormous steam ironing board, there was the big brown radio, always on, the rightmost of its six white Bakelite buttons pressed down for ultra shortwave, the round dial tuned to music, shows, and news. But Uncle Norbert's tailor shop would have been quiet: he worked alone. The first radio show in Germany did not air until Lotte was ten, and most people could not afford a home radio until she was an adult. Sewing for a living meant that not only was Norbert a handy babysitter, but he also needed someone to keep him entertained: The child to whom he could tell stories became a child who would, eventually, tell him stories in return.

As soon as Lotte learns how to read, she spends hours each day reading to Norbert from the newspaper or from books he brings home from the library. I imagine her crouched beneath his tailor's workbench, on the low wooden tailor's stool, a book open on her lap; Norbert will help her sound out the longer words. He'll fold the *Essener Volkszeitung* or the *Essener General-Anzeiger* so that she can read a section appropriate for a young child.

In between readings, Lotte and Norbert talk about what they've learned. As she grows older, Norbert takes her to the theater on weekends, to concerts, or to the opera. The two of them are thick as thieves: between a father who works sixty hours a week in Krupp's steel factory and a mother who is perpetually weak, fatigued, and often short-tempered from heart disease, Uncle Norbert is the adult in Lotte's life who listens and who talks, who calls the doctor whenever Lotte's mother faints, who is always there, always has time.

By the third grade, Lotte has become such an accomplished reader that she is regularly assigned to read to her classmates at school while they immerse themselves in art projects or needlework. Later, her teacher will praise her essays. And Lotte loves to write: the scritch of fountain pen on paper, the stories that unspool themselves in ink, line after line, page after page.

When Lotte finishes school, at age fourteen, in spring of 1927, it is the time of the Weimar Republic, the period when women first start to work outside the home in Germany, mostly as cleaners, shop assistants, seamstresses, nurses, or secretaries. Women also make first inroads into journalism, and some writers, like Irmgard Keun and Hedwig Courths-Mahler, publish the first bestsellers—for the first time it becomes possible for a woman to live on what she earns from her writing. Lotte sees the bylines of female reporters pop up in the *Essener Allgemeine Zeitung* or the *Rheinisch-Westfälische Zeitung*. And she adores Hedwig Courths-Mahler's serialized novels, eagerly awaiting each new installment.

⋘ ⋙

Perhaps it was Uncle Norbert who suggested that, if Lotte wanted to write, she might try to find work at a local paper. As it happens, just four years earlier, the *Rheinisch-Westfälische Zeitung* had opened its offices and a newly built printshop in the Reissmann-Grone-Haus in Essen's Sachsenstraße, less than a half hour's walk from Lotte's family's apartment. I imagine Lotte showing up at the busy printshop, maybe in response to a "help wanted" ad, with a recommendation letter from her teacher in hand. All the reading she has done has made her a spelling and grammar whiz, so, along with washing coffee cups, running errands, and feeding paper into the printing machine, she is hired to read page proofs before the trays of finished type are screwed into the press.

Picture teenage Lotte there: a short slip of a girl in a building full of grown men. In the foreman's office above the printing floor, she bends over a small desk, her feet propped on a rung of her chair, pencil in hand, tongue sticking out as she concentrates on marking typesetting errors, the ink on her proof sheets still wet. Large windows connect the typesetter's office to the workshop below, where men are lined up in rows, throwing lead slugs of type into trays. Beyond them, the press stands silent, its open maw hungry for the evening edition's type.

How much of what Lotte proofreads is she taking in? Two years earlier, Hitler was arrested, sentenced, and jailed for his coup attempt in Bavaria. Right-leaning judges freed him a few months later. Within a year, he published *Mein Kampf*, created the SS as his personal bodyguard, and refounded the Nazi Party. What is Lotte thinking about a paper that pontificates about the "superiority" of the "German Race," that propagandizes the right of this "superior race" to displace "lesser peoples"? A paper that is purporting to represent workers, like Lotte's father, but is really targeted at well-to-do steel barons, and which soon transforms itself into a Nazi propaganda machine?

Below the windows that line one office wall, Lotte's corrected spellings are being set in lead. She watches the foreman hand over the sheets, watches the bent backs of the typesetters, watches their arms fly as they sling letters, plop, plop, plop, into the setting frames. These men, these whirling arms, are framing what's to come, feeding the presses, day after day, pounding stories into brains.

What is happening to Lotte's brain here? There are the leaden letters, day after day, the proof sheets, the still-wet ink. There is her pencil, hovering, pouncing, picking away at punctuation marks, at faulty typography, but never, never straying toward faulty propaganda lines. Lotte wants to stay here, by the letters, by the press. She wants to be sent out on assignment, to write. But, day after day, her brain grows heavy, dull. Day after day, Lotte's head droops, drops, sinks onto the proof sheet on her desk. She startles awake, looks up, wipes drool from her cheek onto her sleeve, stares down at ink smeared across her once-clean shirt. She jumps up, runs to the bathroom, gazes at herself in the small, spotted mirror above the sink. Brown curls. Huge blue eyes. She turns her head to try and read the ink stamped across her cheek: propaganda's mirror image, imprinted across teenage skin. *Führer*. *Weltherrschaft*. She is a walking advertisement for

Hitler's words, printed in reverse. Sometimes, to find mistakes, you have to read a sentence back to front, the mirror showing you what's really there. *Herrenvolk*. Oh God. She cannot stay. She wants to stay. She wants to write. She wants to be Hedwig Courths-Mahler, hold onto her pencil, to the press, the print, the make-believe stories of female heroines holding out against the odds, her words flying, flying, as paper unspools and unspools.

Watch Lotte return to her desk, face wiped clean, sleeve still damp. Watch how she hunches over her proof sheet, her feet hinged on the rung between the chair legs because they don't quite reach the floor. Slowly, slowly, her head begins to nod forward, her eyes close. She'll jerk awake, focus on the letters beneath her pencil stub, until her head begins to sink again.

Eventually, the foreman shakes her shoulder. "Lotte," he says, "child, wake up."

She startles, looks at him bleary-eyed, then wipes a dribble of saliva from the corner of her mouth. After months of watching her, the foreman still can't believe that anyone can fall asleep like that while the press on the other side of the office window is shaking the house.

The typesetters, busy slotting the evening edition into place, don't look up. Lotte looks down at drips of drool on the green rubber mat that covers her desk. "Sorry," she says, "it's only been a minute."

"Lotte, we've got to talk."

A frown gathers her eyebrows, her eyes turn determined. "It won't happen again."

"You know you can't promise that. Look, Lotte, you're a bright girl. And I know you really want to keep working here."

"Then don't fire me."

Are the typesetters' heads jerking around? Or is the press's rumbling loud enough to cover up her sharp tone?

Lotte softens her voice. "Really, it won't happen again."

"I don't think you can control it," the foreman says, "or else you would."

It feels wrong to the foreman that he has to shout this to make himself heard. But the printing press is so loud there is no quiet place in the building to have this talk.

"I've watched you; you don't fall asleep like other people. And you've already told me you're not staying up late at night."

Lotte shakes her head no. They've been here before. She's getting plenty of sleep, she says. And he knows she really wants to be here—she's waiting for a chance. And why not? He's seen it happen for plenty of the guys: Running odd jobs for the press office one day and then, bang, they're sent out for their first story when two workers' marches happen at once and nobody else has the time to cover the opening performance of the new play at the Grillo Theater that day.

She thinks she can write, and maybe she can. He can count on her to find the missing punctuation, switched letters, spelling mistakes. But this isn't the place for her. Perhaps if she were in the newsroom upstairs, not down here, right above the press. But her assignment isn't something he can do anything about; he needs her to feed paper into the ever-hungry press—and he has seen her head nod forward as her hands go slack too close to its lead-toothed maw.

"Lotte, it just takes some people that way. It's the lead. The air down here is full of it. And if you keep breathing it in, you'll only be getting worse."

She looks like she's about to cry, but she's got to know.

"This is the third time just today. You've been getting worse each month. It's not right to keep you on."

He can see her swallow, pull herself together. She won't cry after all. She's quick, she's funny, she's got spunk. The men will miss her. But she can't stay.

"We've sure loved having you here," the foreman says.

I don't know why the foreman was so certain that Lotte's sleepiness was due to lead exposure—despite narcolepsy being a relatively rare condition, he might have seen symptoms of lead poisoning in enough of his workers that the conclusion seemed obvious to him. We still don't know how exactly lead can trigger narcolepsy in genetically susceptible people—one theory suggests that it destroys brain cells that produce a neuropeptide called hypocretin, which is needed to prevent daytime sleepiness.

Lotte's next job is in what she referred to as Haus Bethanien—I believe this may have been a residence for elderly ladies. Together with other girls, she cleans rooms, makes beds, serves meals. Her sleepiness follows her there. Often, she feels so bone-tired that she sneaks up the attic stairs, plops down on a wooden step, and falls asleep, her head propped against the banister. The only reason she does not lose her job is because one of her friends keeps watch for their supervisor, races up the stairs, and shakes Lotte awake before her absence is noticed.

I don't know how long Lotte works at Haus Bethanien. It is the middle of the Golden Twenties, when the Dawes Plan helps the German economy boom, unemployment is at a historic low, and theater, music, and literature blossom. But the economic upswing in Germany is not shared by steel and coal workers in the Ruhr area, where strikes for fair wages and a shortening of the sixty-hour work week prompt steel barons to order massive lockouts and layoffs. Two hundred and forty thousand striking workers are fired. Over the next several years their unions win, over and over, in the courts, but the Weimar government is powerless to enforce court decisions against the owners of coal mines and steel factories. As a result, a quarter of a million families in the Ruhr region descend into utter poverty. I don't know if Lotte's father was among the workers who lost their jobs, but if so, the family would have subsisted on meager aid from the union, the supplement to the rent they received from Uncle Norbert, and whatever Lotte might be able to earn. By the time the conflict ends, Lotte is sixteen. Soon after her seventeenth birthday, the Great Depression hits, American banks call in the credits they extended to German companies, and the German economy collapses.

Sometime during these turbulent years, Uncle Norbert opens a tobacconist's store. Standing behind the counter is hard for him, so he hires Lotte to help run it. The store window displays expensive cigars, but mostly Lotte sells "looseys"—individual cigarettes, bought by young men who are out of work. Alfred, her future husband, will meet her that way: buying a cigarette or two when he has pennies to spare. Over the next twelve or thirteen years, Lotte will get pregnant, marry Alfred, and survive war, displacement, hunger, and five Cesarean sections. There will be no time to write. Alfred will be wounded in the war but, unlike so many other husbands, he will eventually come home. Lotte will feel grateful that he does, that she has what so many women all around her will crave all their lives: a husband who is alive, who will do anything to keep the family fed and safe. For the remaining decades of her life, she will worry about Elfriede, Anna, and baby Alfred, the three children who survive their births: all of them restless, driven, unable to sit down, to be still and breathe, unable to listen, always on the go.

Only after Alfred's death, alone in her small apartment, will Lotte finally sit down with her daughter Anna's discarded appointment books. She will pick up the pen she dropped so long ago. She knows the story she wants to write: the dreamy coffee-in-the-garden scene, the yarns in pink and baby blue, the husband who comes home from work, shared joy about a pregnancy.

But Lotte's reading to six-year-old me stopped with her protagonists' embarrassed, joyful smiles. If she wrote more, those pages failed to make her vicious cut for the boxed-up anthology of old letters and miscellaneous documents she left behind in the two drawers of her rolltop desk. I never asked what happened to the happy couple in her story after she read to me. I don't know if the wife finished the baby sweaters, or if they saw their children born and grown. Perhaps Lotte's writing stalled because the story had been set in her present-day 1970s, when an ultrasound told women not just about their baby's health but also what color yarn to buy. Perhaps a story starting in a garden where women knitted, unafraid, a place where husbands returned home from work instead of war, could not carry a plot. Perhaps she stopped because the real story—of fear, of friends who disappeared, of leaden letters, marching men, of deportations and concentration camps, bombs and hunger, loss and cold—this real story could not be told.

schweigen, v.

Imagine if silence were something you did, instead of something you heard (or didn't hear). In English, the verb *to silence* takes a direct object, someone or something to be shut up. In German, *to silence* is intransitive: something you do, but not something you can do *to* someone.

Der Wald steht schwarz und schweiget, goes a still-popular German song, written by Matthias Claudius in 1779, about the risen moon: "The woods stand black and silent." Except that these woods, in German, do not "stand silent," they "stand *and* silent," as in an action, and what they do, as they stand, is to emit no sound, convey no message; they fail to chatter or to sing. Their *schweigen* is not a refusal, it is an act.

WHEN WOMEN WRITE

ENGLISH IS MY GENERATION'S second language, but it is not my mother's. English is the shovel with which I can dig for her childhood, scrape it up from the bomb cellars, the railroad tracks, the muddy bottom of a pond—and keep it secret from the people who might ask her questions were they to read it, to see. English means my mother doesn't need to worry about what her friends and neighbors will say.

My mother's fear of gossip makes sense. When she was a young child in Nazi Germany, what the neighbors said could get you harassed, locked up, or killed—Party informants were everywhere.

I learned about the silence that such spies can cause when I was in ninth grade, on a class trip to Eastern Germany. My teacher admonished us, sternly, before we crossed the border that, if we said anything to arouse suspicion or annoy Eastern German officials, our words could land us in jail—and he'd be unable to help us. Even the most raucous classmates went quiet on that trip. I remember riding on public buses full of East German adults and schoolchildren who sat in their seats without speaking to each other at all. What someone overheard one child saying to another on a bus in Eastern Germany could send their parents to prison, the children to a state-run orphanage. The silence of such bus rides, of quiet streets inside any totalitarian regime, can burrow deep beneath your skin, weave concertina wire around your throat, build inhibitions you never learn to shake.

Growing up in Western Germany meant that I learned not Russian but English in school, passed my TOEFL test in college, and was eligible for a Fulbright grant, which paid for my first two years in an American graduate school. A few weeks after I landed in Portland, Oregon, the Berlin Wall came down. It wasn't something I'd thought I would live to see. And though I told myself that there was, of course, no logical connection between my leaving for America and the fall of the Iron Curtain, it felt as though, somehow, there was: America was big, and I could breathe, and now everyone I'd left behind could also breathe.

In Oregon I lived in English, new tracks that ran on English words building inside my brain, creating an English "me" who learned new rules of being, far from family and old friends. While German-me took yearly visits home and penned letters in tiny script on tissue-thin blue airmail paper, English-me was busy learning the words I needed to be a scientist. And yet my journals, my way of processing emotions, stayed in German through these years. When, maybe a decade later, they flipped to English for a while, I came back to German with a jolt of shame: Writing in English felt like a betrayal, like giving up on who I was. English was not how my mother would have told the story. English was not how to tell my story to myself.

But English became the way I told my story in 2003, nearly fourteen years after I first came to the US, on a walk through late-March woods in Pennsylvania, where I had moved to teach college biology. Under bare-branched beeches, my friend Laura thrust her cane down as she walked and said: "And this morning I open up the newspaper to a picture of this woman staring at her house." Her free hand swung in a wide arc for emphasis, painting the entire scene.

I knew immediately what photograph she was talking about. It showed an apartment house in an Iraqi city that had been hit by a US airstrike, its front wall torn off, the rooms and their furnishings exposed as though it were a dollhouse.

"I saw my grandmother in that picture," I blurted out, before I could control myself. "Both of my grandmothers."

"What do you mean?" Laura stopped, turned to me, both hands finding the top of her cane, spring sun sparking her copper curls.

And so, for the first time, in English, I said that both of my grandmothers had seen their houses bombed, that they had fled from burned cities, with small children in tow, after massive bombing raids.

It wasn't something I talked about with my German friends. In German, the story was self-evident. It lived, unspoken, beneath nearly every family.

Since I'd been in the US, I'd learned that the American lens on World War II was from above: brave fighter pilots and their bomber crews evading German flak and air defense, their "carpet bombing" paving the way for heroic US troops to win the war.

But here was this American photograph from the ground, this woman in her black headscarf staring in disbelief, the photographer having turned his gaze from male bravery to women, to torn-open homes. And here was Laura, leaning on her cane, wanting to know what it meant to see my grandmothers in this image.

Throughout my childhood, Oma Lotte's stories dropped into my hands like balls of tight-wound yarn. The yellow porcelain bathtub cools my bottom as I watch Oma dip a comb in beer, pull it through a strand of her hair, roll the lock around a plastic curler, and jab it into place with a steel pin: "Your mother once flushed the bathroom key down the toilet." Or, her voice drifting down beneath the faux-marble couch table, keeping me entertained as I dust the ornate legs with a goat-hair brush: "One day, we almost couldn't get to the doctor's office because there were huge bomb craters in the road." Or, while I hang over the vinyl back of a kitchen chair, frowning as she slips a row of half-formed eggs from a chicken carcass, catching them in an enamel bowl: "We used to joke that we needed to take your mother around to see all the relatives before her eyes grew shut—she was such a fat baby." Or, more than a decade later, after I tell her about a friend's bed rest during her pregnancy: "The doctor told *me* I should go to the hospital immediately, but I said to him: 'I've known this child is dead for weeks; another few days won't make a difference.' How has your friend been holding up?"

Laura listening, under Pennsylvania beech trees, leaning on her cane, was how I began to tell, and later, too, to write, how I began to let my grandmother's words seep from German into English, from one world into the next, from small-town Germany into small-town Pennsylvania, from German-me into English-me. Laura's wide-open eyes, her wanting to know, opened a door between two parts of me, making a passageway for stories I had heard as a child and teen.

Around the anecdotes, something else would crystallize: an English cup to hold the passed-down moments, the passed-down words. A framing. An understanding built from words that made up the adult, not-German, part of my brain, the words that had learned to take apart the world and reassemble it anew, to look for connections, for other people's stories, for literature, for science, for numbers and dates and history: English words. Words my mother would not recognize. Words in which to catch and serve my mother's childhood to the world.

For years, I looked for English words as though they were loose keys inside my purse: the tools I needed to unlock the spasm of cricopharyngeal muscles in my throat that blocked feeling from rising into speech. Eventually, digging and digging through the frayed lining, the silences between generations, English flipped the whole thing inside out to find that what I needed was never the key but instead, one of my mother's bobby pins from a beehive hairdo fiftysomething years ago, my grandmother's U-pin, escaped from a plastic curler, my great-grandmother's hatpin, its decorative peacock feather miraculously still intact.

-<<<<< >>>>>-

The English words to hold my mother's and my grandmother's stories never come without hesitation. Laura's parents fell in love on a US Navy ship, traveling from Africa to Italy at the end of the war. Her mother was a nurse, her father a supplies officer. Writing in English means to write for children and grandchildren of men and women who helped to defeat the army in which both my grandfathers served. It means writing to the liberators of the concentration camps.

How can I ask my American friends, much less total strangers, to open up space in their hearts for a woman fleeing burned-out Essen with two tiny girls in tow when, in that same city, Jewish people were arrested and killed and American POWs were worked to death in weapons factories? How can I expect anyone to feel for children and young mothers in a country that carried out genocide on a previously unimaginable scale and began the most violent and deadly war in human history? The answer, each time the questions rise, is that I can't. Except: Here is Laura, wide-eyed. And Laura wants to know about my grandmother staring at her ripped-open house. And here are all my grandmother's story snippets, bumping against the insides of my mind like a bar of soap floating in a bath. As insistent to be picked up before they dissolve. And just as slippery.

"I can't" keeps popping up in every essay, every draft: What on earth am I doing, writing about Lotte's shattered dishes, my mother's whooping cough, her fear of cats? How many Jewish children in the gas chambers? How many Russian soldiers dead?

I tell myself that my grandmother's stories must already be out there: they aren't new. There must be novels that tell this tale, that will show me how the women of my grandmother's generation lived through the war. In looking for these stories, I discover that I am not alone in my hesitation to write about German suffering. In 1997 the German-born writer and professor W. G. Sebald gave a series of lectures in Zurich, which were published two years later in *Luftkrieg und Literatur* (and later, in English, in *On the Natural History of Destruction*). In these lectures he accused German postwar novelists of letting Germans down by failing to write novels about the bombings of Germany. Where were the stories, the spellbinding characters to bring readers into the bombing raids? Sebald posited that there was "a kind of taboo like a shameful family secret" that had prevented German authors from writing stories about individual suffering during the war.

There followed, upon the publication of Sebald's lectures, a debate about whether it might ever be appropriate, or even possible, to write about German suffering in the way that a novelist is supposed to write: by bringing the reader into an experience without immediately relativizing or explaining it away in light of the greater suffering caused by Germans themselves. The question never arrived at an answer.

And maybe what was happening to me was also what happened to Sebald, too, in England, which he visited as a lecturer in 1966, at age twenty-two, and where he then lived from age twenty-six until his death: He wrote in German, but he lived in English, wrote his German words about memory and Holocaust and war for an English-speaking audience, surrounded by English-speaking students and colleagues and friends. His novels were largely unknown in Germany, but

English readers bought and loved his translated books and, finally, brought him recognition, even fame. And maybe from that English perspective, from the other side of the Channel, from the place where people wanted to know, arose the question that no one else had asked, or maybe never asked as effectively: Where were the stories of the wounds left by the bombs?

In response to Sebald's lectures in Zurich, others, like Volker Hage, the literary editor of the German magazine *Der Spiegel*, dug deeper into the books that had been published by German authors who lived through the war. They pointed out that there *had* been German authors who had written novels about the bombings, but that, unlike Kurt Vonnegut's *Slaughterhouse-Five*, the work of German authors—written in German, for Germans—had been ignored and forgotten: There had been not so much a lack of writers, but a lack of German readers for German writers' work.

But when I dig through the stories unearthed by Hage and other literary critics to help me understand my mother's and grandmother's experiences in the war, I come up short: the writers they discuss are near universally men. Then, as now, the people who survive or die in bombing raids are mostly women and children.

Hage, too, noticed this: "German postwar literature was mostly written by men," he said to Sebald in an interview in 2000 in Berlin. He then asked: "Might this also explain why certain topics don't appear at all?"

In response, Sebald recounts an anecdote in which a famous German writers' group, during one of their first postwar meetings, decides to visit a bordello as a kind of joke, dragging the only two female members, the poets Ingeborg Bachmann and Ilse Aichinger, along with them for the event. Bachmann, one of the most important German-language poets, would have been twentysomething at the time, which means she would have survived the war as a teenager. But instead of wondering what young Ingeborg might have written had she been in different company, Sebald ends the story with a note of dismay about the bordello incident ("It makes your hair stand on end, even forty years later"), without telling us what he thinks the absence of women writers from the literary canon means for literature.

Ingeborg Bachmann's hometown in Austria, Klagenfurt am Wörthersee, was bombed fifty times over the course of the war. She would have been eighteen during the first major attack, on January 16, 1944, when three waves of US planes dropped about 1,200 high-explosive bombs on the city, causing 234 deaths and critically wounding 73 people. Out of a population of maybe 100,000, 1,800 were suddenly without a home. By the end of the war, over 60 percent of living spaces in the city were destroyed. When I look for anything Bachmann might have written about her teenage experiences, I find her lyrical short story "Jugend in einer österreichischen Stadt" ("Youth in an Austrian town"), first published in 1960 by *Die Zeit*, a major German news magazine. The piece lists some of the things that children are "allowed" to do during the war:

> During alarms, they are allowed to leave their exercise books and go to the bunker. Later, they are allowed to save candy for the wounded or to knit socks or weave bast fiber baskets for

> the soldiers, for those of the earth, those of the air, and those in the water. And to commemorate them in an essay, under the earth, and on the ground. And even later they are permitted to dig trenches between the cemetery and the airfield, which is already bestowing honors upon the cemetery. They are allowed to forget their Latin and to learn to distinguish the motor sounds, to calculate the area that a low-level attack fighter plane can cover with bullets. They no longer have to wash that often; nobody is concerned about their fingernails. The children mend their jump ropes, because new ones can't be had, and they converse about delayed-action detonators and Teller bombs. The children play "Let the robbers pass" in the ruins, but sometimes they only squat and stare and fail to respond when someone calls them "children." There are plenty of shards for playing "Heaven and Earth," but the children are shaking because they are drenched and cold.
>
> Children die, and the children learn the dates of the Seven Years' War and the Thirty Years' War and they would not care if they confused who was whose enemy, the causes of and reasons for, the exact distinctions between which will earn you good grades in school.

My mother was too young to go to school during the war. But still—Bachmann's cynical casting of the wartime breakdown of rules that govern children's lives as "permissiveness" gets to me, exposing the distractedness and absence of adults who might keep children safe. My mother, too, remembers being sent out to play, with the added instruction for all children to "dive under the apple trees" if they should hear a plane. She, too, at four or five years old, was expected to perform the split-second calculus that let her identify a strafer from the pitch and rate of change in engine sounds.

Where was teenage Ingeborg during the attacks on Klagenfurth? What did she see, hear, fear? Which "children" died? Who did she lose? "Youth in an Austrian Town" keeps the experiences of the bombings at arm's length—not only does Bachmann choose a male character through whom to tell the story, but she makes him narrate a collective childhood trauma, not a specific experience. In the fellowship of other German authors, most of them men, there would have been nothing unusual about Bachmann's own youth amid falling bombs, nothing that could be processed within a community of writers who insisted that the only purpose of literature was to counter and reject fascism—not to narrate or integrate or feel through trauma that any Germans might have endured. Writing in German, for Germans, meant that Bachmann lacked a sympathetic or even curious audience with whom to process her own childhood experience.

Adult Ingeborg's life remained restless and chaotic, as she careened from one country and love affair into the next. Thirteen years after publishing "Youth in an Austrian Town" she died from injuries sustained in a fire caused by a cigarette. A friend visiting her shortly before this accident discovered that her entire body was covered in scars from cigarette burns—burns Bachmann failed to notice because her long-term habit of barbiturate use had rendered her insensitive to pain. Doctors attempting to treat her for injuries from the fire failed to understand her convulsions as symptoms of barbiturate withdrawal. Bachmann likely died as a result. How might her life have been different if English had not just been something she stumbled through the one summer she happened to come to America but a place of refuge, of friendship, of open ears and hearts?

In her book *Trauma and Guilt: Literature of Wartime Bombing in Germany*, scholar of German literature Susanne Vees-Gulani asks whether novels that take their readers into the experience of the bombings could help their writers, but also society as a whole, to process the devastation of German cities. She cautiously singles out books by Dieter Forte—especially his 1995 novel *Der Junge mit den blutigen Schuhen* (The boy with the bloody shoes)—as potential healing stories of this kind. Forte acknowledges the value of the writing process for his own emotional health. The resonance of his public readings also leaves no doubt that his novels initiate processing of memories in his readers: "I received a flood of letters," he said in an interview with Volker Hage, "mostly from women, who were, after all, the primary witnesses of the bombings. Less from men. It is an experience of women, of the war generation of women. Horrendous life confessions, pages long."

Just like the women who wrote to Forte, grandmothers all across Germany told their grandchildren stories about what happened to them in the war. In interviews, women have given eyewitness accounts about the bombings of Germany. Women also wrote millions of wartime letters, and they wrote diaries; some of these have been published. But most women's novels on the bombs remain unwritten, or unpublished, or largely unrecognized.

What about the thesis implicit in Hage's question to Sebald, then, about stories lost if we do not hear from women about the bombs? What does it mean to hear from a writer like Wolf Biermann about holding onto his mother's back as she swims through a Hamburg canal in 1943, away from the flames through which they have just walked—but not to hear from a mother who saved or lost her child? What does it mean to read in Gert Ledig's novel *Vergeltung* (*Payback*) how a rape in a basement buried under rubble turns into an act of love—but not to hear a woman's account of an assault during a raid?

The absence of women's stories from literatures about war is, of course, not a German phenomenon, nor is it limited to World War II. It is global. It seems perpetual. Maybe—just maybe—a reporter asked the Iraqi woman who stared at her ripped-open house in 2003 what she felt or what this meant for her and her children. Maybe a reporter gave her answers a line or two in a news piece that went around the world. Or maybe she was not allowed to talk to reporters. Maybe her granddaughter, too, will wonder what the war was really like: how her grandmother lived through it. What she felt. What women wanted. What they feared. What they did next. How they survived. And what they saw. What are the chances that the Iraqi granddaughter will find a country and a language that permits the telling of her tale? When will civilian experiences, the pain and grief of noncombatant people in South Sudan, in Gaza, in Ukraine, take up equal space with news of, as Bachmann puts it, "who was whose enemy, the causes of and reasons for, the exact distinctions between which"?

⋘⋙

Desperate for women's voices, I start collecting books and stories by German women who already, habitually, publicly wrote before they gathered up their children, birth certificates, and the family silver and headed down the basement stairs. I find Marieluise Fleißer, poster child of German realism, whose short stories make the basement floor jump and buckle under your feet as you hope like hell that the flimsy ceiling will hold. She walks you through rows of POWs plotting to take over the ammunitions plant where you are forced to stare into a microscope all day while you live in constant fear of being taken away by the Gestapo for your published work. I find Ingeborg Drewitz, whose schoolgirl protagonist secretly delivers food and clothing to Jews and communists in hiding as she scurries amid bombs falling on Berlin. I find Johanna Moosdorf's protagonist, who is so desperate to save her Jewish husband from deportation to a concentration camp that explosions and conflagration turn into mere background. And I find silence, suppression, collapse of what could have been descriptions of bomb cellar experiences by women authors who might not have had resistance work or Jewish friends and relatives to legitimize their right to write about the war—a shrinking of descriptions into mere hints, the horror only visible in the characters' estrangement from their postwar lives.

"The insanity that befell my entire generation is the consequence of events we couldn't handle," Marlen Haushofer writes in *Die Mansarde* (*The Loft*), a novel about an Austrian housewife and artist who suddenly becomes deaf upon hearing an air-raid siren. "That's why it is so important to be patient with each other, to watch every word, and to live as though nothing happened. [My husband Hubert] never told me about certain times in his life, times that I spent in the air-raid shelter and he spent in the trenches. His entire life he has worked on forgetting these things; so how could I fault him for growing a little odd in the process? Our youth and the good fortune of survival allowed us to ignore this for a few years. But we did not remain young and I failed first. Hubert, by the way, never would have written about his misfortune, for which I feel obliged to admire him greatly."

The "failure" Haushofer's narrator laments in herself might have been physical: the hearing loss that makes her unable to function in polite society. Or it might refer to her failure to remain silent about her suffering, having let her frustrations spill into written words. Her sense of "obligation to admire" her husband's silence seems to imply that neither her silence about the war nor her admiration of that silence comes naturally or easily.

The unspoken and undesired pact of silence about wartime trauma between Haushofer's narrator and her husband feels familiar. Of the hundreds of letters my grandparents wrote back and forth during the war, only a fraction survive: Alfred, like many German men serving at the front, regularly burned Lotte's letters and asked her to do the same with his. Of the letters Lotte saved, against Alfred's will, few touch upon the bombing raids Lotte lived through—and when they do, they only ask about specifics of what was damaged and express hope that she escaped. There is no acknowledgment of her revealing anything about what her nights in the bomb cellars might have been like. Similarly, Alfred's letters reveal almost nothing about his own experiences at the front. In response to Lotte pressing him for details, claiming that she's heard terrible things from friends whose husbands told them more, he responds that there is no point in writing "such letters"—that the only point he needs to convey is that he is doing fine.

This domain of silence about the trenches and the bombs continued even after Alfred returned home. When I was ten years old and he lay dying from lung cancer that had spread to his bones, his morphine-induced dreams made him scream as he relived scene after scene from the front. But he would never tell Lotte or my mother what he saw. It was only when my father spent an afternoon alone with Alfred that he spoke of the war; my father told my mother that Alfred had shared some of the experiences that were haunting him—but that he was not to repeat what he'd heard. My father has kept his promise to this day. It is as though the men in my family, just like in Haushofer's *Loft*, agreed that silence about wartime trauma and atrocities is the only means through which continuing on as functional human beings can be assured.

The Loft, published in 1969, the last of her many works, is the only novel in which Haushofer, who lived through the bombings of Vienna and Graz with two infant sons, mentions the bomb cellars. She died of bone cancer in 1970, after years of considering her worsening symptoms to be psychosomatic in origin—dismissing the life-threatening signals from her body as an "oddness" of the mind, an expected price to pay for keeping quiet about the traumas of war. My mother says Alfred's cancer diagnosis seemed to pop up out of nowhere—how long he may have dismissed or ignored his own symptoms we can only guess.

Unlike my grandfather's categorical refusal to speak about the front lines, my grandmother's silences lived in what she left unspoken in her anecdotes: yes, she'd tell me about the bathroom key my mother flushed, yes, the water from the overflowing tub running down the stairs, but not my mother, jumping up and down on the bed the night before as Lotte desperately tried to get her dressed to carry her down the basement stairs; yes, the bomb craters in the road, but not the sirens, not the shaking basement walls, the falling plaster, the people singing, praying, screaming next to her; yes, the foreman's words at the newspaper about how lead leached from the type might make fourteen-year-old Lotte ill, but not the words that rolled off the press she helped to feed.

I remember feeling sometimes puzzled, sometimes scared by silences I could not name or describe. The feeling came most clearly on Lotte's blue corduroy fold-out couch in her guest bedroom, where she would put four-year-old me down for a nap, lying beside me, promising a story that would help me sleep: Lilly, the little angel, embarking on a sailboat that would take her far away. Lilly's boat tacking against the wind, into a sunset that— And then my grandmother's whistling snores, her lips shuddering on the out-breaths as I stared and stared, not daring to wake her up, wondering what might yet befall Lilly or the boat, feeling left behind. Awake. And alone.

The blue corduroy couch, my grandmother's labored breathing, her snores, my inability to understand why I felt scared in the safety of my grandmother's guest bedroom—they all come back to me as I read Ilse Aichinger's novel *Die größere Hoffnung* (*Herod's Children*). In one chapter, little Ellen has bought poison at the request of her Jewish grandmother, but now decides to hide it to prevent her grandmother from suicide as they await the Gestapo's arrival at their apartment. In the end, she promises to give it back if the grandmother will tell her a story in exchange.

> "A story, Grandmother!"
>
> But do new stories exist? Aren't all stories old, ancient, and only the jubilations of embracing humans recreate them, the breath of the world? As Ellen demanded a story from her grandmother, she demanded—from her grandmother and inside a dark, dangerous night—the will to live.

But Ellen's grandmother, in that "dark, dangerous night," never can get beyond "Once upon a time," and exhausted sleep finally steals over her, making her a stranger to the little girl.

> "Hello!" said Ellen, unsure of herself, and then placed her warm face against the cold one on the pillows. The gasping sounds calmed slowly, the breaths came more easily. But everything else remained far away.
>
> "Then," Ellen said, resolved, "then I will tell the story."

Aichinger watched her beloved Jewish grandmother being carted off to a concentration camp. After the war, she quit medical school when she could not stop writing *Herod's Children* in a frenzied attempt to record what she had seen during the war. It was Aichinger's first novel and—as for Haushofer and for so many women after her who wrote about their experiences —it was also her last. In an interview with *Die Zeit* on her seventy-fifth birthday, she claimed that, once she saw her book in print, it seemed far too long to her: "I would have preferred to say it all in a single sentence." Though she never went back to medical school and writing became her career, the pieces she wrote subsequently grew shorter and shorter. "Even as a child," she says in the interview, "my greatest wish was to disappear. It was my first passionate wish. I can hardly remember anything besides that crazy wish. The wish is still there."

My Oma Lotte was not Jewish. No one took her away to die. And yet my body knows Ilse Aichinger's wish to disappear. The wish lived in my stomach, its hot hands twisting and digging, all through my childhood and my youth. It still rises, a familiar visitor, swelling, threatening to suffocate me, as though my own existence feels complicit in creating suffering in the world.

At the end of Marlen Haushofer's *The Loft*, the narrator regains her hearing as she listens to a wartime criminal confess his atrocities. The silence of German writers about the suffering civilians endured in the war feels inextricably linked to this: Facing our own families' pain can never be uncoupled from the greater hell our people caused. There is no healing from trauma without taking on a burden that feels too large to hold.

German holds my grandparents' silences—my grandfather's categorical resistance to speaking about what he did and saw, the gaps between my grandmother's anecdotes. On the other side of a vast sea, English is a place of freedom, a place to see anew, a place to unpack and hold my mother's and my grandmother's splintered memories, to spin the threads that may make them cohere; to get away from old proscriptions about what can and cannot be said. English words are safe from my mother's friends and neighbors—and from her. English is a walled garden into which my mother can only gain entry if I open a door, opt to translate for her: a plot of deep, dark soil where my voice can grow strange thorns and tendrils, safe from the shears of my mother's anxieties. English is made of words my mother never told me not to say.

Brandbombe, n. f.

A backhoe in the woods near Stuttgart scrapes once, clearing leaves, twigs, black soil, yellow clay. A member of the bomb squad pulls apart the excavated soil with gloved hands, then grabs a shovel. Together with a younger colleague, he digs up a slender metal canister, corroded, maybe three feet long. They heave it from the hole.

"Brandbombe," the younger squad member explains.

Incendiary. Literally: "Firebomb." A metal can that reeks of gasoline, raw rubber, and a host of other as yet unidentified flammable materials. Built to ignite, then splatter, stick, to keep burning in myriad nests on rafters, on the furniture of busted-open rooms, designed to be dropped after a first wave of "blockbuster" bombs has knocked clay tiles from roofs. Not meant to be swallowed by soft-damp soil.

But here it is. Beneath this shady woodland path upon which little old ladies in long wool coats walk their Yorkies and Maltese: the stench of hell.

BURN SPIRITS

THE BOTTLE'S EMERALD GLASS shines from the back of my grandmother's kitchen counter, the fluid inside it crystal clear, the label white, its print unreadable to four-year-old me. I stare at the bottle. My Opa Alfred has just put it down. The feeling in my stomach turns from thirst to queasy pain.

My grandparents' green glass bottles of mineral water live in plastic crates, in the basement. My grandfather usually carries the bottles up the stairs, returns them downstairs empty. One or two always sit on the counter in case someone needs a drink. But now Opa has not brought the bottle up from the basement. He has carried it inside from the balcony.

I often wake up thirsty. I often become thirsty throughout the day, intensely, desperately thirsty, gulping down water until the tingly-empty feeling in my belly goes away.

Very early this morning, I had padded across the kitchen's gray linoleum in predawn light. I stood on tiptoes, reached, found the green bottle with my fingertips. No one else was awake. I could hear my grandparents' breathing through their bedroom door across the hallway: my Oma Lotte's nasal whistles, my Opa Alfred's sonorous snores. I knew not to wake them. The bottle scooted across the Formica counter, down into my hands, full of clear-cool-wet to soothe the pit beneath my ribs, the middle-upper-belly hole. I've learned to call this hole *Durst*, the German word for "thirst": its need of something, anything to push against its itchy, cramping hollowness from inside out.

I'm not supposed to drink straight from the bottle. But I know how. This morning, I was in luck: someone had already popped off its sharp-toothed metal cap. I lifted the cool glass bottle with both hands, pressed its hard-smooth lip against mine, tipped it, and sucked at prickly bubbles, drinking deep. Again. Again.

But now I stand and stare. Petrified. Minutes ago, the bottle flashed green in noontime sun when my grandfather took it out onto the balcony. He admonished me to stay inside, closed the sliding glass door. He poured clear liquid from the bottle over the charcoal on the grill, then lit a match. Flames shot up, huge, blue-red. He twisted the cap back onto the bottle, stepped back inside.

"Opa, how did you make fire with water?"

"This isn't water," Opa explained. "It's Brennspiritus."

I stared at the bottle, the white label. *Brennspiritus*. I tried the word against the stinging fizz my grandparents' carbonated water always made inside my mouth: "Burn spirits." The German word for denatured alcohol. It made sense.

"Can I drink some?"

"No. This is poison."

Opa tightened the cap once more, set the bottle onto the counter, pushed it far back, against the wall, then picked up the plate of bratwurst and carried it outside.

Sun pours through the kitchen window onto the bottle. It glows. Deep in the hole beneath my breastbone, death digs in its claws. An understanding dawns: Taking what my body wants will kill me.

Time is so big when you are small. Minutes pass like hours as I walk around in shock. The prickly burn beneath my sternum grows and grows. When it becomes unbearable, I tell my grandfather, in tears, that I drank from the green bottle while he slept.

He takes one look at me and laughs. "If you'd really drunk from this bottle, you'd be dead by now." He walks out of the kitchen, to do whatever he meant to do next.

It sounds logical. I understand. I am not dead. There is no trip to the doctor. No hospital. I didn't throw up. This means I cannot have drunk *Spiritus*. Opa would know. He would. My brain says this, over and over. But the bottle is green. Green. And the tummy place, the hole beneath my rib cage, screams.

For weeks, months, years it will flare, whenever I am undistracted, at rest, alone: the deep suspicion that I swallowed poison, that I am sick, will soon be dead. And that telling anyone about it will not help. For years, my brain will try to tell my belly: No hospital. No doctor. Not dead. For years, my belly nerves will screech: yes, but it burns, it burns, it burns!

What did the hole beneath my rib cage need but never get? Why couldn't my grandfather pick up a bawling four-year-old, hold her, wipe away tears, ask her how she felt, ask why? Why could his lanky body not warm, soothe, wrap up mine, his breath and voice and presence, his knit shirt against my cheek, his tobacco scent seeping into me, calm and safe? Why could he not listen, then show me that there were two kinds of green bottles, pop the crown cork from the one, twist the cap off the other, let me sniff, first, the nothingness of water, then the warning sting of alcohol?

Much has been written about the men of my grandfather's generation: how they went away to Hitler's war, killed and looted, burned. How they did not return, or returned with shrapnel in their bodies and missing arms or legs, missing comrades, missing teeth. How they came home to bombed-out houses, flattened cities, to news of friends and relatives dead or lost, to wives and children they no longer knew. How they missed their children's childhoods, never learned how to hold and soothe and talk. How war had taught them not to feel but act, to put the bratwurst on the grill, to do the next thing to stay alive.

What fire, what burning spirit, did I swallow? How does war turn water into flames inside a child's mouth?

schweig, v. imp.

Schweig' stille mein Herze!—"Be silent, my heart!"—commands the last line of every stanza in Eduard Mörike's poem "Schön-Rohtraut." The heart to be hushed in this romantic poem from 1838 belongs to a young boy who has fallen in love with Rohtraut, King Ringang's willful daughter: a pretty princess who refuses to spin or sow but instead gallops through woods and fields, hunts and fishes. By the third stanza, she asks the boy for a kiss—and gets it. This love is, of course, doomed, because the boy lacks standing to ask for Rohtraut's hand. But beneath all the imperative heart-hushing that ends every stanza, there is the memory of this moment of self-permission, this kiss: a bouncing joy that survives all repression.

In German, the imperative "*Schweig!*" commands someone to *do* something. In English, "Be silent!" asks someone to *be* a certain way. I want to believe the German is only meant as a temporary injunction against a heart's telling. I want to believe that the English is not an actual request to give up who we are.

RED CURRANTS

SHE STOPS IN MID-GREETING, mid-step; I nearly bash into her knees with the picnic basket swinging from my hand.

"What's wrong?" I ask, balancing the willow-wrapped handle across my left forearm to rummage through blanket, coffee flask, fork, spoon with my right, making sure the bag of sugar is still wedged upright, between the currants and the white enamel bowl. She doesn't answer, doesn't move. I look up into her face. She gazes past me; I turn to trace the line of her fixed stare. The entrance lodge to the Licht- und Luftbad looks the same as always: red geraniums, peeling paint, tack-bitten wood around the ticket booth window cluttered with signs—women this way, men that way, admissions prices, rules and regulations, opening times. Even the porter is the same.

"What is it?" I ask.

Sweat trickles down my neck. My head feels fuzzy, as though in supplication to this fifty-sixth day of unrelenting heat. Shadows bloom across her face, her eyes expressionless beneath black bangs, the skin across her cheekbones blanched under its summer tan. She shifts her weight and gives a little shake, as if to rouse herself.

"I can't go in."

It takes another minute, too many seconds, for my eyes to swivel between the entrance booth and her face. Too much time for a thought to drop.

"Oh."

She turns slowly, away from the entrance. Away from the sign. My delight to see her here again, today, fades to confusion. My brain flicks through images, in search of sense: A deluge of air- and light-filled afternoons. The woman's slender shape in the sunbather's dress, long arms flying skyward, her fist hitting the leather ball dead center. The sparkle in her eyes as she turns to her team, punches the air: "There, we've shown them!" The hours—how many?—of rest in grassy shade, my picnic blanket spread in sight of hers. Stolen glances, in between the fork's glide along pale-green stems. I look up from the translucent red of currants pinging into the enamel bowl to let my gaze rest on her eyelids, trace lashes, the curves of her arms and chest, the wild flood of her hair. Each de-stemmed berry's single drop of red into its white crystal bed, hurried spoon-scratch—I scramble to my feet to follow her into another round of ball, leaving berries to bleed into their sugar coats. Returned to the blanket, breathless from play, I spoon and chew as, three paces away, her graceful gestures straighten her dress, re-pin her hair. Inside my mouth, coated pearls explode acid, gritty crunch of half-dissolved sweet grain pulp of seed and skin.

Since the days grew hot in June, I have hauled a pound of currants through each sun-soaked afternoon, my sandals slapping across sidewalk pavers awash in broiling heat, twenty minutes from the corner grocery by my parents' rental apartment, down block after block of workers' housing to this green oasis. After days of gloom and dust, of selling cigarettes, three at a time, to men and boys who can't find work, this is where I come to breathe, to laugh, to be at ease in women's company. The Licht- und Luftbad is my refuge away from home and town, from voices on the radio.

The basket drags against my arm, imprinting braided willow onto skin.

"Then I'm not going in either," I say, seeking her eyes. She nods once, then turns away. I blink through tears. I do not need to read the bold-faced print, the words not meant for me, already too ubiquitous. Two lines, four words. JEWS NOT WELCOME HERE.

My Oma Lotte told this story again and again. Currants brought it on. Reminiscences of hot summers. Deliberations on the merits and dangers of sunbathing, discussions on the value of ball sports for girls. Each time, her Jewish friend's beauty bundles the story's light. Never a name, never an indication that the two of them talked more than to acknowledge each other in greeting. Each time the shock at connecting the sign to a face, the instant decision not to go in: a burnt fuse, a breaker thrown, lights out. Sometimes my own eyes see the letters from the sign outside the Licht- und Luftbad. Sometimes my retinas and taste buds feel like my grandmother's rather than my own. Though she lived and told this story, it feels like mine.

Red currants glow inside a basket. A white sign on brown wood. Black letters slap a label on black curls. My grandmother stood, stunned. She turned and left. She did not return. Then, she got pregnant.

Less than six months after this last visit to the Licht- und Luftbad, still living with her parents, and without the financial wherewithal to start a household, my grandmother, Anna Sophie Philippine Charlotte, conceived my aunt Elfriede, her first child. Lotte hadn't only just met Alfred; they didn't make a baby in a lovestruck burst of pheromonal fog. Alfred was part of Lotte's group of male friends. By mid-December of 1936, she had been dancing and flirting with these men for years. Despite the admonitions from her mother, Sophie, who habitually snapped at Lotte's two busybody, namesake aunts, Philippine and Charlotte, Lotte was never alone with any of the men—there was safety in numbers. But Lotte wasn't stupid, inexperienced, or seventeen—she was an adult woman, twenty-five years of age.

By the time Lotte got pregnant, she would have known Alfred for at least four years. I know this because Lotte repeatedly told me about a fight in Uncle Norbert's tobacconist's store that nearly ended their friendship in 1932. I have tried to imagine what that fight might have looked like for Alfred.

"I can't believe you voted for him!"

The contrast between Lotte's bright-blue eyes and the dark brown of her bobbed curls never fails to startle Alfred. Growing up short has made her feisty, with opinions on exactly everything. For years now, he has hoped she'll pick him of all the unemployed young men who hang around the tobacconist's. The other night she slipped her hand inside his elbow as the group of friends had walked her home, after the concert in the park. Had it been dark by then, who knows, maybe she would have let him kiss her as they said goodnight in the deep doorway of the apartment building where she lives with her parents on the second floor.

Today she flings his coins into the register, slams the drawer shut.

"He's the only one who can do it," Alfred says, unfurling his long spine.

He has been done with school for years. There is no work. Not for him. Not for his older brothers. Never enough to eat for his six-foot-one-inch appetite. And no way out of his parents' cramped apartment, out from under his father's iron-fisted rule. No way to sweetness, warmth, to his own family.

Lotte says nothing. Red circles flare on her cheeks.

Alfred turns abruptly, away from the ice in Lotte's eyes. But at the door he turns and draws a breath: "Hitler will make Germany great again."

The bell tied to the door swings in a helpless jingle, the glass reverberates inside its frame.

Four years after this fight in Uncle Norbert's store, Lotte sneaks Alfred up to her bedroom. Her parents are asleep down the hall. When they hear Lotte's mother ask her father for a fresh glass of water, as she does every night, Lotte and Alfred hold their breath as Lotte's father pads by her bedroom door, to the kitchen, and back to bed. By the end of February of 1937, Lotte knows that she is pregnant.

Of all her male friends, Lotte most enjoyed spending time with one, whom she described as *ein Süßer*—a "sweet man," meaning he was gay. With him, she felt relaxed because she didn't need a plan for when and how to say no. They just had fun together: at concerts, dancing, hiking, talking about books and films. Until the day he was gone. *Abgeholt*—"taken away," the code word for being picked up by the Gestapo or SS.

I regret that I don't know his name. I think she may have said it once, and I failed to take it in. Forgot. Willi, perhaps. Or Heinrich. Or Karl. I do remember that he had brothers, parents, a close-knit family who cared.

I don't know how old I was when she first mentioned him—old enough to know what *abgeholt* meant. Past my first history lesson on the Third Reich. At least in the third grade. Old enough, for sure, to remember a name, or to ask: "How did you find out? What did his parents do?" To ask: "What did you do?" To ask: "Were you scared?"

I never asked. I listened. I listened to her stories of red currants and of her friends as I had listened to her tell me about Lilly the angel—nap-time tales of a grandmother's imagination. I knew that Lilly, though she had a name, was invented. I knew the Jewish woman, nameless, was real. The gay friend was real. I listened the same, no matter whom she was talking about—enthralled, as though listening to music. Just taking the words that came my way, tucking them in, out of sight—each gleaming splinter wrapped, with care, into the folds of a child's soft and winding brain.

Many years ago, in the basement of a northern German university, I took a class on using the electron microscope. To thin-slice plant tissues for its high-resolving beam, I made knives by breaking blocks of glass, creating blades much sharper than steel but also much more delicate. I was taught never to touch the cutting edge, that putting your finger there not only slices skin but blunts the blade, renders it useless. I want to know what the story fragments my grandmother passed on to me meant to her, how they fit together in her mind, rather than in mine, what shape they made within her thoughts, her memory, her life: were they a vase, a mirror, a window, a drinking glass? Did the discovery of the sign at the entrance to the Licht- und Luftbad really happen when I imagine it did, before my grandmother became pregnant? How long before or after that did her gay friend disappear?

Summer in the city of Essen was unusually warm in 1935, unbearably hot in 1936. By 1935, in all of Germany, Jewish people were banned from public swimming pools. But the Licht- und Luftbad was not a pool, just a walled-in green space with two partitions, split by sex, where people played on the grass and rested under trees. Its counterpart in Frankfurt-Niederrad, the only one for which I can find records, claims it was the last one to close to Jews, in May of 1938. So: no later than the summer of 1937 for the currants. Not before 1935. Most probably July or August of 1936.

Twenty-six thousand men were imprisoned by Nazi police for "punishable incidents between men"; over 100,000 were questioned, brutally; 15,000 found themselves outside of the legal process entirely, in concentration camps, where heavy labor, harassment, and torture through medical experiments killed 60 percent of them. The law that made this possible passed in 1935, but police and storm troopers had already closed gay bars for both men and women long before, in February of 1933. In 1934, the Gestapo sent telegrams to local police ordering lists of men with "known homosexual activity" to be mailed to Berlin. In 1936 the criminal police became part of the Gestapo under Heinrich Himmler, who had been running Hitler's concentration camps since 1934. That year, many gay men and women married, some emigrated, some committed suicide. From early 1937 to mid-1939, 78,000 gay men were arrested. By the time my grandmother got pregnant, the knowledge that something could happen to her friend would have hung in the air like a poisonous, sticky fog. Likely, he was already gone.

Alongside the words, expressions, anecdotes, my memories catch on Oma Lotte's tone of voice. I can still hear her swooning over female lawyers, chief secretaries, doctors, authors, and once, a baroness: *Eine tolle Frau!* The German adjective *toll* lives on tonality. English dictionaries toss up "neat," but "neat" conveys some distance, a judgment that separates the speaker from the spoken-about. *Toll*, in German, is unrelated to the English: it knee-buckles in admiration, waves a lighter at the concert stage, dances in the streets with joy. It is forever starstruck, drunk on hormones, twelve.

Despite her rapt descriptions of her Jewish friend's beauty, I don't believe my grandmother considered that she might be sexually attracted to women. But if she thought about this, would I know? And, more vexing still: Would she have known to label her attraction as anything? The term *lesbisch*, "lesbian," only entered common usage in German in the 1970s. Was love between women even really talked about in the coal mining cities of the Ruhr during the 1930s? Based on the records I could find, antigay Gestapo activity in Essen seemed to target mostly men. As a teen, I too knew about gay men—the neighbor who regularly came to my parents' store to tell my mother about his aging partner's cancer and his grief. But women living together flew under the radar, were assumed to be cousins, sisters, friends.

Although women were not explicitly included in Nazi antigay laws, some lesbian women did end up in concentration camps. Rather than the pink triangle gay men were made to wear on their chests, these women wore a black one, labeling them not as "gay" but as *asozial* or *gemeinschaftsunfähig*—"antisocial" or "incapable of living in community." There remain large gaps in research about the Nazi persecution of lesbian women. The current consensus seems to be that most Nazis assumed less outspoken gay women could be forced into marrying men and giving birth to babies for the Führer's war. As long as they kept silent and played along, these women survived.

Change was slow to come. In 1957, the German supreme court ruled that Paragraph 175 of German criminal law, which forbade same-sex relations, was "insufficiently related to Nazi law" to necessitate a reconsideration. This ruling kept same-sex relationships illegal until 1969, by which time 50,000 men had been sentenced to up to six months in prison and another

50,000 had to endure court proceedings that did not result in sentencing. The criminal police continued to maintain "pink lists" of gay men until 1978. Marriage between same-sex partners only became legal in Germany in 2017. The German Bundestag finally held its very first memorial event for gay victims of the Holocaust in January of 2023. Through my early adolescence, love between women remained implicitly illegal in my home country—as safe as it was invisible.

Germany, of course, is not unusual in holding onto anti-LGBTQ legislation. Sixty-four countries still uphold criminal laws against same-sex relationships; in twelve of these, the death penalty can be imposed. As of mid-May, 2025, the American Civil Liberties Union is tracking 575 anti-LGBTQ bills across 49 US states—a situation that will likely worsen with further implementation of Project 2025.

I have a single photograph of Alfred and Lotte on their wedding day: they sit ramrod straight in matching armchairs. Several tall vases hold flowers on the floor by their feet. Both look serious, staring straight ahead, off-angle to the camera and to each other, an arrangement that might have been staged according to rules of photography at the time. There is no white dress—perhaps because there was no money to spare, or perhaps because wearing white was supposed to symbolize that the bride was a virgin, which my pregnant grandmother was clearly not.

Despite the solemn photograph, I have no doubt that my grandmother loved my grandfather. My grandparents accomplished more than a lasting marriage, more than mutual care, more than raising three children in terrible, frightening times: through thirty-four years of marriage, they talked about their feelings. I know because I heard them speak to each other. I know because my mother heard them too. I know because, later, my grandmother told me about some of their conversations. And I know because of my grandfather's letters sent from the Russian front—letters about the two of them, brimful of emotion: love and longing. Anger, homesickness, and fear; humor, jealousy, grief, pain—and returning, over and over, to love. Their marriage didn't skirt emotion. They lived it.

Why, then, do my fingers on the keyboard keep tripping into acid sugar, currant red, into my grandmother's sandals on hot pavement stones? What makes her story mine to feel, to tell?

Maybe it is mine because she ached to write and never did. Maybe it's mine because I was there, with her, listening. Listening after my grandfather's death, listening each time Oma Lotte worried where Elfriede might be or whether she was well or ill, listening when my uncle and my mother were so intent on building safe and ordinary lives that, each time my grandmother began to speak about the war, both of them jumped up to do something else, something that needed urgently to be done exactly then—my uncle, usually, to play his guitar, my mother to make more coffee.

This story is mine to write because I stayed at the coffee table. It is mine because of shared hours of folding sheets and towels, of stripping currants for jam or cake. It is mine because she told me, because it stuck with me. Maybe I listened differently from everybody else.

I met my husband in graduate school, en route to a seminar about the genetics of wild sunflowers. That's my story. He says the seminar was about butterflies.

After several failed relationships with men, I was determined to live happily on my own in a tiny studio apartment plastered onto the side of the oldest house in a small town in Oregon. Like me, the house was a transplant: it had been moved into town, close to the university, from its original site by the Willamette River. Inside its walls, I lit tea lights, rolled out my yoga mat, worked hard toward solitary contentment. But every Wednesday night, on my drive home from a shift at the local food co-op, I cried. I told myself I was just tired.

Hummingbirds buzzed by my apartment on their way to the neighbors' *Ribes sanguineum*, Oregon's native currant bush. Forget-me-nots grew around its wooden stoop. Because of the butterflies, it soon had two people living within its 250 square feet. A botany professor called our arrangement "a grafting experiment," tissues forced to fuse by proximity. We easily agreed on taking turns standing to dress or cook and sitting on the bed. After I defended my PhD and before my visa expired, we married so that we could both live in Germany. Nearly twenty years later, I fell in love with a woman.

Breaking up my marriage felt exactly like untangling grafted hearts—life-threatening surgery, the hardest thing I ever did. We grieved. We stayed friends. My mother said she hadn't wanted to mention it before, but it had bothered her from the beginning that my wedding picture shows one of my hands balled into a fist. My husband's smile is rapt, and I smile in return. But my fingers obey a different line of emotional control. My husband only discovered the fist after we separated, while leafing through old wedding photographs. It made him cry. I had noticed it immediately when the pictures came back from the developer. But the part of my brain that noticed such things had a habit of fainting into the next armchair instead of making itself heard. Maybe this part of me didn't know what to say or how to say it. Maybe another force within my psyche kept it choked. Until I tried to write about my grandmother eating red currants at the Licht- und Luftbad in 1936, about the disappearance of her gay and Jewish friends, I did not understand that this choking might be a safety switch.

The year before I moved to Oregon, its voters passed Ballot Measure 8, which repealed the governor's regulations to shield gay people from discrimination. The repeal enabled landlords to evict tenants based on their sexual orientation and employers to fire them. I had moved to Oregon in 1989, but I first heard about Measure 8 in 1992, when the Oregon Citizens Alliance put forth Ballot Measure 9, which, if it had passed, would have declared homosexuality "abnormal, wrong, unnatural and perverse" and required all schools, public universities, and government branches to expel gay employees.

After that election, I walked around in shock. It felt physical, a slug to the gut, an intensity I couldn't label or explain. My fellow graduate students and coworkers pointed out that there was no reason to be dismayed: Measure 9 had been defeated, after all. Fifty-six percent "against" was a resounding victory, they said. But I could not stop counting off strangers in the street, wondering who had voted "in favor." Forty-four percent, to me, looked very much like nearly half—just about every other person. My stomach clenched, yet my head soothed me with stories of how I was dating men—my horror was sympathetic, someone else's, the threat of expulsion never about me.

Two years later, Measure 13, banning books by or about gay people from public libraries, failed even more narrowly, by a little under 19,000 votes. A fellow graduate student and her girlfriend spent a night in a protest camp on campus, just around the corner from where we worked in our labs. Someone took potshots at their tent. I was outraged and shaky. And still, I told myself my rage and fear were only about threats to my friends and favorite books.

Over the years that followed, I saw three doctors for inexplicable exhaustion, brain fog, stomach and kidney troubles. My diaries from this time despair over fatigue and inconclusive medical exams, but never once mention the election. I wrote pages and pages about feeling safe inside my relationship with my boyfriend, alternating with desperation over not wanting sex. Not a sentence about feeling attracted to women. No memories of such thoughts. But there, on an empty page, apropos of nothing, a newspaper clipping, a grainy black-and-white photograph of a painting by Hans von Aachen from 1604: *Die drei Grazien* (The three graces), which depicts three women standing nude, in a triangle of interlocking arms, arranged to display breasts, thighs, bellies, buttocks from the front, the back, the side.

Women don't need a grandmother who came of age in a fascist state to be blindsided by a first same-sex attraction in midlife.

There are books about this, scientific studies, online discussion groups. Some hypothesize that late-onset changes in sexual orientation arise from hormonal shifts. Some propose that being attracted to one sex for part of our life and another at a different time is a function of sexual fluidity, that this is how humans are made, and that only culture induces us to think otherwise. One of my friends claims that all women are sexually drawn to other women but that few of us dare to live that attraction.

I thought women being more attractive than men was just how things were, objectively. I remember a moment on a college trip: a shared bathroom, glancing into a large mirror over a row of sinks. Behind me, a curvy fellow student stands naked, the perfect Renaissance nude. She waves her hands, raves about a man she met. "Wow," I thought. "I can really see what that guy must see in her." But I don't remember thinking about touching, about anything beyond the pleasure of this stolen glance.

My mother says my grandmother kept secrets. A day or two after I tell her that I've fallen in love with a woman, she calls me on the phone.

"I've remembered something," she says. "After the war, your Oma Lotte used to take me and Elfriede to see two of her friends. We called them 'aunts,' but they weren't really related to us or to each other. They lived in Essen, so we would sometimes take the train to see them when your grandfather was out of town."

Images of a trip with my grandmother rise in my mind. "Did they live in a very small apartment?" I ask. "In one of those giant apartment blocks with a lawn in the center? Was there a bathtub in their kitchen, with a board on top, so that it worked like a kind of counter?"

"Yes," my mother says. "Yes, that's how it was. And whenever she took us, she said we absolutely could not tell your grandfather where we had been."

I ask her what she means.

"Your grandfather was very jealous," my mother reminds me. "I now wonder if those women were a couple. I know your Oma Lotte was fiercely fond of them. And your grandfather would get really angry when she mentioned them. Each time we went there, she was adamant that we could not tell him."

Some of Alfred's surviving letters from the Russian front might hint that his attempts to curtail Lotte's time with women friends began early in their marriage: there are angry admonishments that my grandmother spent too much time in conversations with other women instead of writing to him about more details of her daily life. Some letters reference other—missing—letters, drawn-out written fights.

Later, I remember that Oma Lotte took my sister and me to see the "aunts" soon after my grandfather passed away. I would have been ten or eleven, my sister nine or ten. When I call my sister to ask about her memories of that trip, she describes being fascinated by a photograph in their apartment, showing one of them in a fancy dress and swooping hat: young, beautiful, glamorous—an actress, my sister thought.

Was there one bedroom in that no-room-to-turn-around apartment? Were there two? Who were my grandmother's women friends? What were they to each other and to her? All I know is that the very moment I told my mother I had fallen in love with a female friend, the forbidden childhood visits to the "aunties" rose immediately in her mind.

My sister once walked by the Licht- und Luftbad with our Oma Lotte, when they took a trip together to find the house where Oma grew up. Deep in the workers' quarters of Essen, close to Krupp's steel factory, they trudged through streets lined with apartment buildings, each square block of houses shaped around a central lawn, green space originally designed for spreading laundry to bleach in the sun, now turned into playgrounds.

I ask my sister whether they met with any of Oma Lotte's friends while they were there.

"No," my sister says. "Remember, she was the only one who got away."

I frown. "Away from what?"

My sister says the Licht- und Luftbad was where my grandmother met her Commie friends.

"Her Commie friends?"

"The KPD folks," my sister says. "Her group of friends. They had regular meetings to do Communist things."

"Communist things like what?"

"Like learning Esperanto," my sister says. "Except Oma Lotte never learned, because her mother forbade her to go to the evening class. It wasn't political, she was just against her daughter going out at night; she wanted to have her home."

My sister says our great-grandmother Sophie's possessiveness spoiled Lotte's fun but saved her life: The Gestapo used the Esperanto class roster to find and deport her friends.

"Deport? Like, send abroad?"

"No," my sister says, "*deportiert*. Like, *abgeholt*."

While I had wondered when my grandmother lost her gay friend, her beautiful Jewish friend, I had never imagined that the rest of her friends had been sent to concentration camps too. I had never considered that in December of 1936, when she conceived my aunt, her one remaining right-leaning friend, my grandfather, might have been the only one of her friends who remained.

I have checked my sister's story: the Licht- und Luftbad as a place where women might have secretly talked politics. Exercise grew into a common pastime during the industrial revolution. Cycling, soccer, and gymnastics clubs were class-segregated nearly from the start, leaving workers to establish their own. Because Nazi philosophy saw physical education as a way to demonstrate Aryan supremacy, even left-leaning sports clubs initially remained untouched by *Gleichschaltung*, the alignment of all public life under Nazi ideology. During the first few years after Hitler rose to power, some exercise establishments in working-class neighborhoods developed into hubs of Communist or Social Democrat resistance. In between ball games, women plotted how to slip money and food to families of the "deported." JEWS NOT WELCOME HERE killed an island of resistance, a last refuge of political community.

In the absence of federal protections, currants and love live or die by local law. Few Americans know the taste of fresh currants, fewer yet crave it as a taste of home. In Pennsylvania, currants are hard to find, because currant bushes were outlawed in 1933. Several other states had also banned planting of any members of the genus *Ribes* in the early 1900s to prevent a tree disease called White Pine Blister Rust. These days, because most modern currant cultivars carry resistance genes to the rust fungus, Pennsylvania no longer enforces its ban. When neighbors gave me extra currant bushes from their yards, I crossed my fingers that no one would care to resurrect old prohibitions. I planted joy in glowing red. Each summer, robins, chickadees, and cardinals beat me to the harvest, but every remaining berry spills childhood memories inside my mouth.

Hans von Aachen's renaissance nudes have names: Glanz, Blüte, Frohsinn—radiance, blossoming, joy. The choking part inside my soul, the part that plants bright-red danger signs where I might otherwise find joy, the part that won't permit the fullness of who I am, the part that dims my light—I owe her gratitude. I watch Great-Grandma Sophie pull a metal comb, relentless, through Lotte's snagging curls. I hear her throw a fit about her daughter's nighttime Esperanto class, quenching her exuberance, saving her life.

To walk my own path means naming Sophie's voice. It means hearing the sound of Lotte's sandals plodding homeward across hot paving stones. It means the braided willow imprint on the skin below her elbow, the weight of currants, uneaten in her basket, the weight of sugar, separate in its paper bag.

Übersetzung, n. f.

Übersetzung means "translation," but it also signifies how two cogwheels relate to one another: the number of turns one has to take relative to the other, the fact that, if they are to move together, the smaller one will need to spin much faster than the larger one. The closest English translation is "gear transmission ratio."

Note that any geared device can change the speed, torque, and direction of a force.

Note that any word may be a geared device.

"Translation," from Old French *translacion*, first appeared in English in the fourteenth century, when it was used to describe the process of taking a saint's body or relics from one place to another.

In English, the ferrying of a *Blindgänger* from Berlin's center to an abandoned quarry for detonation, then, might be sacred, an act commanding not only concentration but mindfulness, respect.

Similarly, the verb *übersetzen*, "to translate," originates from the Middle High German *ubbarsezzen*, which means "to take something from one place to another." If you stress the first umlaut, it still means to take yourself, or something, or someone across a body of water, such as a river or a lake. Move the emphasis to the third syllable, and *überSETzen* becomes "to translate"—to carry something from one language into another, a meaning it acquired somewhere between seven and nine hundred years later. To be German means to hope that you can take a boat from one language into another, across the Rhine, the Danube, the English Channel: It means that words can ferry you across difference.

In English, the verb "to translate" replaced the Old English *awendan*, from *wendan*, "to turn." The motion here is different: A translated world looks fresh and new because you've changed direction. Before English words were translated, or carried across, they were turned around. In English, translating begins as a switch in perspective, as looking at the world a different way.

SYLLABUS* FOR MY MOTHER

Catalog Number	GerLit 090-490
Academic Year	1948–2019
Course Title	Witnessing Destruction

INSTRUCTOR

Your older daughter. You used to call her "the absent-minded professor," because she kept forgetting her gym bag and her art supplies, because she was happiest inside her head. You bought her books from which to build that internal world, bricks for a fort in which to hide. Your instructor began to catalog books when she was seven, after a friend first led her up the concrete steps to your town's library. She walked into that story scent, the promise of living a thousand imagined lives, ran fingers along smooth spines aligned on shelves, and envied the women behind the counter who could spend

---

* syl·la·bus /ˈ*siləbəs*/ noun: (1) an outline of a course of study. (2) In the Roman Catholic Church, a summary of points, decided by papal decree, regarding heretical doctrines or practices. From Google's English dictionary, provided by Oxford Languages.

their days making order, stamping return dates, writing call numbers in a log. Your younger daughter soon bounced her shoulders off the doorframe to your instructor's room, right, left, right, left, intoning "I'm bored! Tell me what to read!" You started asking that question four decades later, after your younger daughter's children went off to school. By then, your instructor had become a professor in a faraway land, but you're unsure what that means or what she does.

OFFICE

Three thousand miles away. You saw it, once, during your only visit to America, twenty years ago. You remember your astonishment at how there could be so much light at the end of a dark, ugly hallway. You try to imagine your instructor there, backlit by tall windows.

PHONE

When you call the office line, your instructor knows something is seriously wrong. Now that you've figured out how to push the green receiver symbol on WhatsApp, you wait for your instructor to call you instead of calling her. She usually does. You miss her as soon as you hang up, wonder about her after one week, start worrying after two. You never call just because you feel like it—you vowed you'd never press your daughters for calls or visits in the way your own mother hounded you. You feel stupid when you can't find the little camera symbol for the fifth or seventh time. Your instructor will tell you not to worry, but, until her video feed pops open on your screen, you will picture her rolling her eyes.

MEETING TIMES

This hybrid course will be offered in the form of two intensive two-week, in-person consultations during winter and summer breaks. During the academic year, your instructor will be available via phone and WhatsApp.

MEETING LOCATIONS

Car. Dinner table. (You cook.) Bed. Walking path around the duck pond. Ironing board. (You iron.) Doctors' waiting rooms.

CATALOG DESCRIPTION

An exploration of novels by female authors* who lived† through the bombings of Germany during World War II.‡ We will read stories left out of Volker Hage's *Zeugen der Zerstörung* (Witnesses

---

* Until recently, Germany enforced a law that all given names must be unambiguous gender identifiers. This allowed your instructor to make a spreadsheet in Excel, enter the name of each woman listed as a German author on Wikipedia, and spend much of a sabbatical year figuring out which women wrote about huddling in basements as their cities shook and burned above them.

† Wikipedia lists most authors' years of birth and death.

‡ Wikipedia and other websites can tell you where authors lived between 1941 and 1945 and when bombs fell on those cities.

of destruction),* a work often considered to represent the literary† canon‡ on the bombings from a German§ perspective.¶

---

* Volker Hage, *Zeugen der Zerstörung* (Fischer Verlag, 2003). Your instructor read this book in search of the things her grandmother did not tell her about nights spent in bomb cellars with two babies, the younger one of which was you. Your instructor discovered that Hage only included two female novelists: Gertrud von Le Fort, whom he praises for *not* describing the hours her protagonist spends in the bomb cellar, and Ilse Aichinger, whose novel he analyses only from the perspective of Aichinger's Jewish heritage. Your instructor next wrote to Susanne Vees-Gulani, who wrote *Trauma and Guilt: Literature of Wartime Bombing in Germany*, a careful, nuanced analysis, published by De Gruyter, also in 2003. Some of the twenty authors Vees-Gulani studied survived the air raids as adults, others as children. Some of them were persecuted or imprisoned. Most, but not all, were German nationals. None are female. "Did you come across any works by women that describe the air war?" your instructor's email asked. "If so, is there a difference between male and female literary representations?" Your instructor never heard back.

† lit·er·ar·y /*ˈlidəˌrerē*/ adjective: concerning the writing, study, or content of literature, especially of the kind valued for having a marked style intended to create a *particular* emotional effect. See: par·tic·u·lar /*pə(r)ˈtikyələr*/ from Latin, *particularis*: concerning a small part.

‡ can·on /*ˈkanən*/ noun: Old English, rule, law, or decree of the church. From Greek *kanon*: any straight rod or bar, standard of excellence. Not to be confused with can·non /ˈkanən/ noun, from the same Greek root: a large-caliber, mounted gun.

§ Which Germans? (Consider here Ruth Klüger, *Was Frauen schreiben* (What women write), Zsolnay Verlag, 2010, p. 9: *[In women's books] the treatment of women is more respectful, the insights into their intimate lives are more convincing, women are less often relegated to supporting characters, and when they are, these are developed with more nuance and care.*)

¶ per·spec·tive /pərˈspektiv/ noun: (1) the art of drawing solid objects on a two-dimensional surface so as to give the right impression of

PREREQUISITE

A hunger for written words. Remember how your mother wanted you to stay in school? You fled what could have been a college track at age ten. You say you panicked because you couldn't bear the thought of failing your first English class. You'd had to stay home for six whole weeks with, of all things, plantar warts—so bad, so painful, that you could not take a single step. You could not walk toward the words you needed then. Or maybe your feet tried to protect you because they knew you weren't yet ready for the words. Your fifth-grade teacher rode the streetcar all the way to the end of the line, an hour each way, then walked from the stop, another half hour, to your house—all to convince you that you could catch up. You refused, dissolved in tears. School was over for you at age fourteen. Your spirit has been starving since. You sent your daughters out into the world to collect the books for your bedside table and the pillows for your sleep, like mothers before you sent their daughters after herbs for healing salves.

COREQUISITES

SLP 101–103. Taught by your younger daughter, who holds three different diplomas as a sleep expert from bedding institutes in

---

their height, width, depth, and position in relation to each other when viewed from a particular [sic] point; (2) a picture drawn to enlarge the effect of distance; (3) the relation of two figures in the same plane; (4) an attitude; (5) an understanding of the relative importance of things.

Switzerland and spends her days advising customers on the beds and bedding that will best support their sleep. She will scan your vertebrae, test the tension in the slats that hold up your seven-layer mattress, order pillows with numbered systems of support, adjust the warmth and breathability of your blankets and your sheets. Can you take a break from words, trusting that neurons inside your brain will figure out new ways of holding hands, new patterns in their electric dance?

TRIGGER* WARNING

Some stories and images will cause flashbacks, bad dreams, and sleepless nights. You will toss off your special blanket, wonder about yet another kind of pillow, remember things you did not know you knew.

COURSE GOALS

Up to you: Where does it hurt? What feeds you? How much pain is too much?

You had no time to read, yet you lined your living room with shelves and filled them with books. Around age twelve or thirteen, your instructor found your copy of A. S. Neill's *Summerhill*:† a magical Easter egg filled with a nougat of utopias. Who knew that schools were mutable? Who knew that

---

* *Supra* note 7: *canon, cannon, kanon*

† A. S. Neill, *Theorie und Praxis der antiautoritären Erziehung. Das Beispiel Summerhill* (Rowohlt Verlag, 1986).

you could make your own? Sometime around that year, you also dragged your daughters into a back room behind the crafting goods store, into what must have been your medieval town's very first yoga class. A decade later, in America, in graduate school, your instructor ran from lab to yoga studio and thought: *This, this right here, is how I want my school to work—*

- Walk in because you want to learn.
- Take off your shoes.
- Notice the stretch. (Only you can know how far to stretch.) Hold it right there.
- Trust that freedom lives inside the breath, between the pain and flinch. Do you want to hang in a little longer, stretch a little deeper?
- Tell your circling thoughts to wait outside, by your dirty sneakers, like large and shaggy dogs, flea-ridden and faithful.
- Begin again tomorrow. Reopen the frightening book. Always begin again.

LEARNING OUTCOMES

As a result of taking this course, you will:

- Say that sleepless nights of rising memories are worth it, because "so much good comes back with all the bad."
- Learn to distinguish past from present tense.
- Sit through family meals without jumping up and running away to the kitchen.

- Turn around at a restaurant and talk to the couple at the table behind yours when you overhear them say that they, too, never once talked to their parents—or anyone—about the war.
- Tell your best friend, who is in therapy with severe depression, that it's time to tell her therapist not only about her husband's and son's suicides, not only how difficult it is to talk to her distant daughter, but also about what happened on her monthlong trek from East Prussia to the West, when she fled from the Red Army at age ten. You will tell her that you are feeling better now that you have told some stories of your own.

TEACHING PHILOSOPHY

Your instructor has a wish for all people to be free, including mothers and daughters. She learned this from you. (Yes, a child can learn a wish, a hunger for missed words.) You say you learned how to wish for your children's freedom from Mrs. Gerhart, who taught a course on pregnancy, birth, and baby care. Mrs. Gerhart suggested you read Kahlil Gibran*, but what is the mystery that allows us to hear the exact words we need as we read, just at the time when we need them?

GRADING

See teaching philosophy.

---

* Kahlil Gibran, "On Children," *The Prophet* (Knopf, 1923).

TEXTS

These will arrive at your door, in packages from Amazon.de or from bookstores specializing in titles long out of print. The address stickers will bear your name, but your instructor will call before they arrive, so that you won't refuse acceptance of suspicious merchandise you don't remember ordering. She will tell you that the books inside the package really are for her, but that you are welcome to open the box and read anything you like.

COURSE CALENDAR

1948–2011

You know how to read, but you won't read anything that touches upon war. After television appears in your home, leave the living room if the news or any movies mention war. Skip entire sections of the newspaper. Skip reading newspapers altogether. Appoint your husband as Chief Curator of your media content.

2011

Open packages and ponder trigger warnings in the syllabus. Read jacket covers. Say "yikes" and close the box. Put it in the basement until your instructor comes home for Christmas.

2012–2013

Open more packages. Read some more jackets. Don't worry that some of the books you find in there are for kids.* Trust that an author's inner child might write to yours.

Read Asta Scheib,† who turned six in 1945, born the same year as you:

> There was the war. As long as I had been able to think, there had been the war. The war wrapped itself over my head like a potato sack. Everything around me, the houses, the people, seemed to detach themselves from me, became strange, blurry, and finally vanished. I was alone in a kind of chaotic dream, from which I probably still haven't fully woken.

Ponder the potato sack. Ponder the dream from which you never woke. Does it matter, now, to have another little girl your age show you the sack in words? To name the dream as dream?

---

* Yes, yes, of course there's W. G. Sebald, who, on p. 112 of *On the Natural History of Destruction*, brushes off any books written for children as wholly inadequate (". . . I can hardly imagine that a genre specifically for young people had hit upon the right dimensions for description of the German catastrophe.") In the previous sentence he also helpfully notes that he hasn't actually read any of the books "for young people" that Dr. Joachim Schultz of Bayreuth University recommended he might read. Which tells us, mostly, who W. G. Sebald thinks literature should be for.

† Asta Scheib, *Sei froh, dass du lebst!* (Be glad you're alive!) (Rowohlt, 2001).

Read Helga Schütz,* who was eight at the end of the war, just two years older than you. Read how Eli, Schütz's child protagonist, survives the bombings, barely, just like you. How she, too, finds herself in an orphanage. How she, like you, is found, how she, too, has a grandfather who keeps her safe. Like you, Eli feels too stupid to succeed in school, is told to do things during her apprenticeship that make no sense—and finally finds her own way to subvert the rules. There is a way to name the way, yes? Even if there is no way?

Note how Draginja Dorpat† picked nettles for soup, because there was no spinach. Just like you. Notice how being six years older than you helped Dorpat to escape Scheib's "potato sack," to convert chaotic dreams to theory, to push them into thought:

> At first, when the war began, I thought there's always a war, in any century. Wars aren't anything special. As soon as one is over, the next one starts.

At eight, your instructor, too, had theories on war. She deduced that all humans had to survive one war within their lifetime. She thought that you were lucky that you had gotten yours over with when you were small. She waited for *her* war to hit. An eight-year-old girl inside your instructor's mind is still

---

* Helga Schütz, *Knietief im Paradies* (Knee deep in paradise) (Aufbau Verlag, 2005).

† Draginja Dorpat, *Und zu Küssen kam es kaum* (Hardly time for kisses) (Klöpfer & Meyer, 2003).

watching for bombs to start dropping on her house. Your instructor wonders if that girl is you.

Next, learn from Else Hübner* how to use teenage belligerence to push against the war. Listen to Hübner's protagonist, Elfi, complain to her mother:

> I don't want to pray! Never again! Because it makes no sense. Back when the war started, I prayed every night for our soldiers not to die, and for us to win, because our history teacher said one was supposed to. Win, I mean. And I prayed in the bomb cellar for nothing to happen. And once I prayed for an English bomber not to be shot down by our flak. And then he firebombed our house. Prayer never fixes anything. Everyone always says, in church, and you, too, that God is almighty and can do anything. And so what's he doing now? Why doesn't he just end this stupid war?

Notice how Elfi sounds like the conversation with your mother that you never had during your teenage years, in 1950s Germany: the silent time, when no one spoke about the war. Let Elfi help you find the helpless rage you never knew to name, to send it through a voice-box valve, a stream of words to hiss like steam. There is a teenage girl inside you who will use those words to push the lid off fear, who needs this steam to help her stomp from scared to free.

---

* Else Hübner, *Tagträume und Bombennächte* (Daydreams and bombing nights) (Salzer, 1997).

2014

"Mom," your instructor will say on the phone, "I've just read a really great book* I think you'd like."

"That's great," you'll say, "let me grab a pen."

"It has two chapters about the war. But I think you might still be able to read it, because of the way it's written."

"That's okay," you'll say, "I can read that now."

Read how a woman can come of age and act on what she thinks and feels is right, even in the face of wrong. See how chapters IX and X, about the bombings of Berlin, work like a hinge, connecting injustice and the violence of the past to their continuation in the present tense. Learn how you need that hinge—to open and to close. To have the world make sense.

NEVER

Read a single book featured in Hage's *Witnesses of Destruction*.†

---

* Ingeborg Drewitz, *Gestern war Heute: Hundert Jahre Gegenwart* (Yesterday was today: One hundred years of present tense) (Claassen Verlag, 1978). Note that this book has won so many prizes that your grandchildren were made to read it in school. Note that Hage, *supra* note 6, never mentions Drewitz.

† *Supra* notes 6–10. Whose literature? Whose words? Whose particulars, emotions, dreams?

OCCASIONALLY

Mention to your instructor that you'd like her opinion on another text that tugs inside your mind, books you'd love for her to read. Elisabeth Kübler-Ross's bestseller.[*] Rafik Schami's stories[†] of arriving in Germany from Syria, postwar. Mascha Kaléko's poetry:[‡]

Mein schönstes Gedicht	*My best poem ever?*
Ich schrieb es nicht.	*I wrote it never.*
Aus tiefsten Tiefen stieg es.	*From deepest depths up-rushed it.*
Ich schwieg es.	*I hushed it.*[§]

ALWAYS

Send another WhatsApp, or mention, gently, in a video call, that you are almost out of things to read. Know you don't need to stand in the doorway, bouncing off your shoulders, right-left, right-left. Know your message will send your instructor

---

* Elisabeth Kübler-Ross, *On Death and Dying: What the Dying Have to Teach Doctors, Nurses, Clergy and Their Own Families* (Simon & Schuster, 1969).

† Rafik Schami, *Die Farbe der Worte* (The color of words) (Ars Vivendi, 2013).

‡ Mascha Kaléko, *In meinen Träumen läutet es Sturm. Gedichte und Epigramme aus dem Nachlaß* (In my dreams the doorbell keeps on ringing) (dtv Verlagsgesellschaft, 2018).

§ Translation courtesy of: https://lyricstranslate.com/en/mein-sch%C3%B6nstes-gedicht-my-best-poem-ever.html.

scrambling, in the midst of a hectic day, for pages that might mean freedom, or delight. Know she will be feeling, yes, rushed, yes, sometimes frantic—know that, as her fingers chase across the keyboard or brush along the book spines on her shelves, she will always, always, smile.

Angst, n. f.

In German, *Angst* means not "angst" but "fear": a feeling that evolved to protect our bodies from predators, from fire, from tumbling down a cliff, a feeling to help us run, hide, fight, or play dead. *Angst* is elicited by something real. *Ich habe Angst vor Krieg*, literally, "I have a fear of war," is "fear of" bombs dropping from the sky. People on both sides of the Atlantic, by the thousands, take this *Angst* with them to the streets to brandish in a protest march.

Translating *Ich habe Angst* into English ("I am scared") turns fear from a noun, a feeling that you have or hold, into an adjective: a feeling that you are. The English noun "angst" derives from the German *Angst*, but it arrived in English via Freud and Kierkegaard, via psychology and therapy. As a result, German *Angst*—"fear of"—transmuted to English "angst": a state of diffuse, persistent—and perhaps neurotic—worry. During its migration into English, "angst" did not replace the word "fear" but instead found its own niche: it lost its capital, became small, personal, and, as such, dismissible. English "angst about war" is not fear but anxiety, something you take not to the streets but to your therapist's couch. Both *Angst* and angst ask for our courage: one to get us marching, the other to stop and find out who we are.

DROPPED STITCHES

I PIN THE PHONE'S RECEIVER to my ear, run my fingernail down the crack in the silky pine surface of my desk. The movers stacked too many heavy boxes on top of it when they packed the shipping container that carried my furniture to America. Outside my Pennsylvania office window, the sun lights maple trees in carmine, turmeric, rust, and gold.

On the other end of the line, porcelain clatters. My mother has put the phone on speaker and is unloading the dishwasher as we talk. It's six o'clock in Germany, and I imagine the kitchen window behind her filled with early dark. Dad is probably in the living room, watching *Die Fallers*, a TV series about a family farm in the Black Forest practically down the road from where my parents have moved for their retirement. Anytime now, my mother will start arranging rye bread and cold cuts on two plates for supper.

"I'm writing about why Oma Lotte didn't knit," I tell my mother, when she asks what I'm working on.

"You're right, she never did knit," my mother finally replies. "But what can you possibly write about that?"

Until my mother's fingers and wrists gave out, she filled her leisure time with needlework. Afghans. Dove-blue dresses for my sister and for me, studded with white hearts. Stacks of the dreaded woolen underpants. Crocheted place mats in matching sets of eight, miles of cross-stitched table runners, mountains of socks. No one else I know grew up with hand-knit tablecloths in size one yarn—eighty thousand stitches to cover a dining table for eight on holidays. Watching TV at night was not enough: to keep her on the couch, my mother also had to move her hands.

One of my friends, the youngest and only sister to seven older brothers, once accused her mother of using childbearing to distract herself postwar. Knitting might be an easier choice. Or work. Or food. Or books.

"I read murder mysteries, and they do not interest me in the least; I even fail to notice if I've read them before. A single one would suffice for my entire life," Marlen Haushofer, fellow bomb survivor, wrote in her final novel, *Die Mansarde*. "I might just as well drink," her protagonist continues, "or swallow pills, or ask some helpful person to hit me on the head with a hammer every day."

Like Haushofer's hammer or my mother's nickel-plated Addi Turbo knitting needles that send her wrists into industrial overdrive, any method of diversion, numbing, and inducing sleep comes with a variety of side effects.

On a gray morning in March, 1943, my mother, Anna, age three at the time, is in Essen, the heart of Germany's Ruhr industry. She coughs, twisting and writhing, as my grandmother, Lotte, pulls her and five-year-old Elfriede up creaky wooden stairs to a doctor's office on the second floor of a soot-stained house. Blades of light pry between boards tacked across a window on the landing, illuminating slices of suspended plaster dust. Halfway up, the smells of lye from boiled laundry and damp mortar from the basement mix with odors given off by turnips simmering in apartments on the upper floors. Sharp smoke has trailed their skirts from the street—Krupp Steel, the only factory that General Arthur "Bomber" Harris mentioned by name as a target for British raids, stands just a few blocks away.

I wouldn't remember when Oma Lotte first explained to me that her family doctor told her not to knit, if she hadn't retold the lead-up to her explanation so often:

"And who made your pretty sweater, dear?" asked a friendly new neighbor in the village where my grandparents had moved. "Was it perhaps your Oma Lotte?"

"No," I reportedly said, with four-year-old authority. "I have two grandmas. The other grandma always knits, but Oma Lotte is always playing cards."

It was the truth and nothing but the truth. Oma Lotte taught us how to play Mau-Mau, a German version of Crazy Eights, as soon as we could hold cards. She made us plum jam, rice pudding, and covered apple cake with raisins, but not a single sweater, not even a scarf or hat.

My mother also knows this anecdote, my grandmother's embarrassment retold as hilarity. I try to prompt her memory: "Remember, Oma Lotte's doctor told her knitting was bad for her."

Another second passes before I hear a clunk: perhaps the big soup terrine hitting the counter. Three thousand miles away, my mother bursts out laughing. "Your Oma Lotte definitely made that one up," she says.

It's true that Oma Lotte used to tell convenient spur-of-the-moment fibs. Like the one about the kitchen cabinet next to her sink being a dishwasher. She tried that one on me when I was maybe four, on a sunny afternoon that beckoned for a walk instead of kitchen chores. "We'll just load these into our dishwasher here," she said, crouching down on the gray linoleum and sliding the stack of soup plates and the bowl with the sticky spoons onto the cabinet shelves, then shutting the Formica door. "See? We're ready to go."

Who did she think she was kidding? Surely she couldn't have believed that a child itching to get to the playground would care if the dishes were done? Maybe she was playfully assuaging the guilty part of her inner self, asking me to stand in for that little inner voice that nags us not to shirk duty for pleasure. Or did she think I'd prattle to the neighbors we'd meet on our walk that her kitchen was a mess?

Perhaps she was simply teasing me, daring me to challenge her tall tale. I wouldn't remember this episode at all if she hadn't retold it too: "And when we came back from our walk, you headed straight to that cabinet, opened the door, and said: 'There, see? It doesn't work!'"

Being found out might well have been the point of the retelling; maybe she didn't delight so much in her own clever deception but in having a grandchild who would silently watch and follow along on a walk, then triumphantly fling open the door and reveal the dirty evidence.

But unlike the dishwasher tale, the doctor's knitting proscription had failed to strike my four-year-old mind as implausible or odd. Knitting was just one of those things that doctors tell you not to do: "Don't smoke." "Don't drink." "Don't put peas up your nose." "Don't knit." Easy. A medical necessity, like "Don't bend down"—the reason I had to crawl under her living room table to dust its complicated legs for her.

Days after I talk to my mother, I remember that she always ended phone calls or left the room whenever Oma began to speak about the war. Does my mother know her mother's stories? Could she ever bear to hear them?

The doctor listens to the children's lungs, then puts down his stethoscope. Wishing he could feel surprise that the girls are back—again—with whooping cough, the second time in just two months, he seats himself, heavily, behind his wooden desk. Too many of his patients have coughed themselves into seizures, rib fractures, pneumonia, or death.

He sighs, then writes out a prescription for cough syrup and gargling salts. Erythromycin, the first antibiotic effective against whooping cough, will not be isolated until 1952. Vaccinations will not become available until 1953. The doctor does not know what's to come—all he knows, in a war-torn country full of coughing children, is that no medicine truly helps with whooping cough. What will cure these little girls can't be acquired at the pharmacy—or anywhere within a half-day's travel: undisrupted sleep, in dry beds, in rooms that still have windowpanes; vegetables, eggs, and fruit. That's what he sent them away to get, over a year ago, when little Anna trembled so hard and so incessantly. Because she was a plump baby, even then, it was her skinny older sister that people worried about. But you don't have to be malnourished to be scared by bombs. You don't even have to be young.

My mother is sitting in a basket on the floor of a basement during those first bombing raids. Next to her, my Oma Lotte has perched on someone's derelict chair. Neighbors from the other apartments in the building sit on other rickety furniture. My mother is crying; she is twelve months old. She is crying because the house is shaking. The house is shaking because planes from Britain are dropping bombs. Planes from Britain are dropping bombs on Essen because Hitler's Luftwaffe is dropping bombs on London. My mother is crying because she wants to be held when the house is shaking, but Lotte can't hold her because she is holding my mother's two-year-old sister, Elfriede. Lotte is holding Elfriede because the doctor has given her a homeopathic powder, which Elfriede must take as often as possible. Lotte is dipping Elfriede's pacifier into the powder, then sticking it into Elfriede's mouth. In between screaming from the pain of an ear infection, Elfriede sucks on the pacifier. In between sucking on the pacifier, Elfriede screams. The doctor has said the powder may help the purulent fluid in Elfriede's ear to drain. The doctor has said if the ear doesn't open by morning, he will have to cut into Elfriede's head. At two a.m., Elfriede's ear begins to drain. Lotte wipes away the pus. She wipes away the tears. My grandmother does all this in secret, under the blanket she has wrapped around Elfriede and herself. The ground is shaking. The neighbors are praying. My mother is crying. Lotte is praying and wiping. The doctor says the draining ear must be her secret. The doctor knows that other doctors know that ear infections can perforate the mastoid bone and form an abscess in the brain. The doctor has received orders from his local health department. The orders say all doctors must fill out a questionnaire about any child showing signs of being "feeble of the mind." The doctor has heard that children get picked up and don't return. The doctor tells Lotte not to tell anyone. Not ever. No one. Not a word.

For fifty-six years following this doctor's admonitions, Lotte will say that Elfriede does not have a mental illness. Not when three-year-old Elfriede tries to smother baby Anna's screams with a pillow until Anna passes out. Not when Elfriede wants to go to church to pray, pray, pray, at five and six and seven a.m., at five and six and seven years old. Not when she wants to drag little Anna along with her to pray, pray, pray. Elfriede is just fine. Elfriede is just fine when Elfriede insists on becoming a nurse who works not just all hours but all the time: during lunch, before and after work, on weekends, on holidays. Elfriede is just fine when she takes the family's postwar rations—hers and everyone else's last slice of bread—to the hospital to feed patients. Elfriede is just fine when she adopts a child within days after she marries one of her patients; she is just fine when she takes in foster children, one by one, while also having five children of her own, until twenty-eight children sit around the tables in her house.

A few years after the police take these children away, Lotte will confess to my sister: she has always believed that Elfriede developed a mental illness because the ear infection spread into her brain. Twenty years later, I will look it up: an article from 2014 cites a publication in the *British Medical Journal* from 1952 that says that, before antibiotics, the chance of a child surviving an ear infection that had spread to the brain was near zero. Other research papers say the correlation between wartime childhood trauma and manic disorders is sky-high. The history papers say children "of feeble mind" were killed by injections of phenol.

I always imagined my Oma Lotte's family doctor as a kindly, white-haired man, a man she had learned to trust as a young child when he came to her parents' apartment each time her mother, Sophie, fainted from heart disease. My adult mind, awash in dates and books, sketches him as a man whose year of birth most likely sent him to the trenches of Verdun in World War I, into the middle of Remarque's *All Quiet on the Western Front*. He then saw French troops occupy his city from 1923 to 1925, when Germans, long behind on paying wartime reparations, failed to deliver enough telephone poles to France. Too old to be sent to the Russian front in the next war, he had instead to watch the front approach his door.

I don't know about this doctor's stance on the atrocities of Nazi medicine, his beliefs about race, his knowledge of torture and mass murder in the concentration camps. I don't know if he thought about the starving POWs and forced laborers who slaved and died in Essen's steel mills, coal mines, and weapons factories. I do believe he cared about his patients, about my great-grandmother, my grandmother, my mother, and my aunt.

"Mom," I say, "do you remember anything about being in Essen during the war?"

A pause. Then my mother says: "I remember the alabaster lamps. They sat on the nightstands in my parents' bedroom. I must have been maybe three, and I was mad about something. So I took a hammer and bashed both lamps. That was one of the times your Oma Lotte spanked me with the carpet beater we kept in the closet by the apartment door. I did a lot of stuff like that—and then Elfriede would run out onto the little balcony and scream all about it down to your Oma Lotte, where she was hanging laundry in the courtyard below."

The doctor pushes up his glasses, squints. A pudgy three-year-old, Anna now seems a handful—she scowls and whines as she tugs her mother's skirt, trying to make her get back up from the chair on which she just sat down.

Lotte says Anna drives her crazy. Last week, she snatched the kitchen scissors and cut the flowers out of her parents' bedspread. Just yesterday, she'd plugged the tub in their second-floor apartment and turned on the faucet, the water running down three flights of stairs by the time Lotte made it up from the courtyard with the laundry basket. Anna had locked herself in the bathroom, flushed the key down the toilet, to boot. Neighbors had to help break open the door.

"Just this morning," Lotte says, "Anna tossed a whole handful of saccharin into Elfriede's oatmeal."

The doctor shakes his head. Both saccharin and oats are in such short supply. Elfriede really could have used that porridge. Even after the months down south, on a farm in Swabia, she is severely underweight, short for her age. Yet she stands tall, her back stiffly erect, behind her mother's chair, her eyes enormous in the white triangle of her face—the kind of child who will hear everything. The doctor vows to choose his questions cautiously.

He shifts in his chair. There should have been another child. He doesn't know if boy or girl. Maybe Lotte knows, maybe not. It's hard for women, giving birth to a dead baby. To his relief, she pulled herself together after that and got the girls out of harm's way, at least for a year. At least until four months ago, when so many evacuees needed lodging that those who had been away the longest were sent back home to wait for another turn.

One hundred and fifty thousand evacuees left Essen by April of 1943.

"Everything done to Essen broke a record," Jörg Friedrich writes in his 2002 book on the bombings of Germany, *Der Brand* (*The Fire*). "The air war went on for sixty months, and Essen was attacked in thirty-nine of them. Krupp, the main target of 1.5 million tons of bombs, seemed best prepared to withstand the material battle. In the city, on the other hand, a mere five thousand of 65,000 buildings remained undamaged."

Two hundred and seventy-two air raids hit Essen over the course of the war. I check the dates and addresses on letters my grandfather sent from the Russian front. The alabaster lamps must have met their demise between October of 1942 and

March of 1943. Not long after the average number of alarms rose to three per day. Not long before the windows, the dishes, the phone lines, and the water mains broke.

Attacks started with "blockbusters" that Germans called Luftminen, "air mines": enormous, thin-skinned bombs, designed to explode before they reached the ground to break windowpanes and blow clay tiles from roofs. They were followed by phosphorus and incendiaries, Brandbomben, dropped to splatter sticky, burning materials all over exposed beams and curtains, igniting tables, beds, and chairs in busted-open rooms. Finally, high explosives to take out water mains, electricity, and roads, and to obstruct access for fire trucks. Tactics similar to those reportedly envisioned by Hitler, over dinner one night in 1940, when he fantasized about setting London ablaze.

"We sit, crowded together," Erwin Krieft writes in *Feuersturm und Hungerwinter* (Firestorm and Hunger Winter), a collection of eyewitness reports on Essen, published in 2007. "We wait. The bombs fall in quick succession, the light goes out. Plaster trickles down. Cracks in the ceiling. Dust, dirt, the smell of Lysol. . . . Our fear was of the air mines. The blast tears your lungs apart. No blood. Death in a thousandth of a second. The next day they are laid out in a row, side by side, covered with white sheets. Incomprehensible and beyond a seven-year-old child's grasp."

Other reports mention newspaper-covered bodies. Did my grandmother steer her daughters around the dead?

Lotte tells the doctor that she has gone to the National Socialist People's Welfare offices three times already, pushing administrators to stamp her next evacuation form.

The doctor doubts she'll make the list. Posters at every train stop exhort women with small children to leave the city, but something like eighty thousand others have lost their homes in the past few days, just in Essen alone. Lotte's apartment house, though damaged, is still standing.

To get to his office today, she says, they've skirted two new craters left by bombs. For days, the doctor has only climbed the stairs between the reinforced basement, the office, and his apartment; he has yet to venture out after the last attack. The whole idea of patient home visits has turned into a joke—anybody still alive has moved in with relatives or strangers. Even if the phone lines were still working, he couldn't find his patients.

Does my mother's brain hold dormant images of flattened city blocks, streets made unrecognizable by rubble, bomb craters ten or twenty yards across, with such unstable sides that anyone who slides down can never claw their way back up? Childhood amnesia, the unraveling of early memories, usually sets in around the age of six or seven, and, by the end of adolescence, leaves most people without memories before the age of three or four.

"Yesterday, when we arrived here, I immediately took off to find the nearest radio," my grandfather wrote on March 15, 1943, from somewhere on the Russian front. "It was quite a way to get there. The city of Essen is still standing, and so is Krupp—the population has suffered losses. Hopefully you, my dear Lolo, have posted an airmail letter immediately."

That spring, my grandfather sent questions on gray military paper into a void for weeks and weeks. In the wake of the

Wehrmacht's defeat at Stalingrad, his company moved too rapidly for my grandmother's reply letters to find him.

"What about the bombers?" he wrote in letter after letter through the early months of 1943. "What about the children?" "What about the whooping cough?"

All through his monthlong furlough, mid-December of 1942 to mid-January of 1943, his only time home in over a year, his daughters had coughed and coughed and coughed.

Children of my generation were born into peace; we were vaccinated against whooping cough. But, as a toddler, my younger sister proved so bronchitis-prone that one of my parents' shop assistants nicknamed her "Mrs. Barky." My mother left us at her parents' house for weeks, claiming that the air in their village was better than in town. It made some sense—aromas of spruce and fir drifted to Oma and Opa's house across oat and potato fields. But, fifty years postfact, it occurs to me that the air quality *inside* their house must have been questionable at best: Lotte and Alfred smoked so heavily that my father's housepainter friend, who helped with renovations, used to joke that their wallpaper was held up by nicotine.

Were children underfoot simply too much trouble as my parents remodeled the clothing store on the bottom floor of our house? My sister responded to the demolition work with desperate hysterics—"They break my house! They break my house!"—her cheeks cherry red and awash in tears.

Maybe my mother needed her hands free to manage workmen, dirt, and plans. Maybe from amid construction chaos and plaster dust, the countryside seemed like a peaceful paradise, full of the kind of "air" that might transform a hacking, howling toddler into a calm and happy child. Or maybe sledgehammers and my sister's screams and coughing fits shook loose anxieties deep in my mother's soul, buried stories she had never learned to tell.

My mother was never taught about the war in school. Western occupiers forbade the teaching of post-1933 history to disrupt the passing-on of Nazi ideologies. Social science only reappeared in North Rhine-Westphalia's curricula in 1956—three years after my mother finished school. Teachers overcompensated for my generation, assigning the history of Nazism and the Holocaust most years, starting in grades three or four. By the time my fourth-grade teacher told us about how city gas fed the heater beneath our classroom's windowsill, and how we could tell there was no leak because of the tiny blue pilot flame, I had already learned about Jewish children dying in the gas chambers. I spent much of the fourth grade obsessively checking the heater's pilot flame: Was it still on? Was I really sure? Whenever I could pry my eyes from the small blue dot of the flame, I'd stare at the jumpy longest handle of our classroom clock, counting how many seconds I could hold my breath.

I wasn't alone in feeling history lessons settle not just into my brain but into my body, the fibers of my nerves, my gut. Discussions on how to help German children understand their country's history, how to replace diffuse, suffocating guilt and fear with productive thought, continue to this day. Most of the children of my generation failed to connect the horrors we absorbed in school with story snippets we might catch from parents or grandparents at home. My Oma Lotte's anecdotes never meshed with Diesterweg's *Grundzüge der Geschichte* (Fundamentals of history) when I was in school. My attempts to stitch them to histories and eyewitness accounts are recent. My mother, like so many children of her generation, never tried.

The doctor slides the useless prescription slip across his desk.

Lotte picks it up, then hesitates. "Actually," she says, "I was wondering—can you prescribe something for me?"

The doctor scrutinizes Lotte's face, the bluish circles around her eyes. "What do you need?" Sleep, he thinks. Three square meals a day. A break from the raids. Definitely not another pregnancy. They ended up doing a caesarean—her third—to remove the stillborn child; he doubts she'll survive another one. He wonders if her husband has been home on vacation from the front. If she's pregnant, it is early yet—she isn't showing. But she is thin, and the dark skin around her eyes could mean anything.

"Something to help me sleep. Or for the dreams to stop. Except I wouldn't want to sleep through the alarms."

Women's books, diaries, and letters from the war tell a consistent story: The exhaustion of repeated bombing raids leaves room for little more than this moment's survival. Many took pills to combat sleeplessness and fear:

"I only grew afraid of the bomb attacks during the last year," the writer Irmgard Keun says in a 1947 letter to a friend in America, "and the fear grew larger and larger. Once the imagination starts working, all is lost. I incessantly had to picture all kinds of horrors in my mind. I ate *Phanodorm* all the time, to make myself a little sleepy and calm."

Most people became scared much sooner than Keun. In Essen, 457 people—and maybe more—died on March 5, 1943, as 3,000 buildings were destroyed by bombs. Seventy thousand people were left without a home as a result of this one attack. The next heavy bombing on March 12 killed 196 more, rendered another 15,000 homeless. In one of those two raids, my grandparents' apartment was damaged. Another bomb hit the house they had been building since 1938. They never got to live there.

The doctor nods. Even if she isn't pregnant, he can't give her barbiturates—she needs to hear the sirens, get her two daughters dressed and down three flights of stairs. They haven't had much warning lately. Sometimes there has been none. There is no medicine to turn off dreams; everybody would be wanting some. He decides to stall: "What are those dreams about?"

"Knitting," Lotte says.

The doctor raises an eyebrow. "How do those dreams scare you?"

"All these balls of yarn keep rolling away from me," Lotte says. "When I try to pull them in, they roll away faster. They tangle; I can't find the knitting needles. Then, when I find the needles, I drop stitches, and I can't pick them back up. When I wake up, my heart is pounding. And I can't get back to sleep."

"Have you been knitting, then?" The doctor's pen taps the prescription pad.

"The other women always knit, in the basement," Lotte says. "All my neighbors do. They send socks to their husbands at the front." She shrugs. "I thought I should try."

Knitting turned into a moral imperative during the last years of the war as textiles, including hand-knit soldiers' socks and caps in olive gray, poured out to the front. New clothes for civilians became impossible to find. Women's stories of endless nights in bomb cellars are filled with accounts of reknitting the unravelings of garments worn beyond repair. Used yarns were wetted and restretched around the hands of friends or backs of broken chairs, then rewound into tight balls. Pullovers, hats, and scarves sported stripes as tattered fibers broke and remnants from several old sweaters were combined to warm a child.

The doctor pinches the bridge of his nose. "And do you like to knit?"

Lotte shakes her head. "No, not at all. I'd much rather read or play cards with the kids so they're not so scared."

The doctor doesn't ask if she has heard from her husband, or if she knows where in Russia he might be. If he was sent to Stalingrad, there'll be no way to send him socks.

German Military Command belatedly acknowledged heavy fighting at Stalingrad on January 16, 1943. On February 3, German radio reported the 6th Army's capitulation—two days after the last of the German soldiers, starving since November amid dead comrades in the bombed-out city, finally gave up. By then, the Russian army counted more than a million casualties—over half a million wounded, nearly half a million dead. The German count remains unclear to this day: around 150,000 soldiers likely lost their lives in the surrounded city; nearly all of the 91,000 survivors died in Russian prison camps.

The doctor pushes himself up from his chair, habitually glances out the window. Its pane may be the only one on this street, or on this block, that has remained intact. Only a single wall remains of the house that used to stand across the street. Somebody has painted the number 1918, large and red, across this wall: the year of Germany's defeat in the previous war. An act of defiance against the propaganda about winning this war, one which could have resulted in instant execution.

He turns to Lotte, who is gathering children, coats, and hats. "Listen to me," he says. "This is my prescription: You are not to knit. Take a book with you. And a game for the girls. Tell your neighbors I said knitting is bad for you."

"Oma Lotte told me the doctor made her stop knitting because it was giving her bad dreams," I tell my mother on the phone. I imagine the kitchen's fluorescent light, her movements reflected in the blackness beyond the windowpane.

"Well, yes," my mother says, "she had a lot of those. You did too, when you were small. I don't know how many times I found you wide awake when I'd check on you at night.

You'd tell me you didn't want to go to sleep because of scary dreams."

"Yeah," I say, "and then you'd leave the bedroom door open a crack, so I could see the light in the hallway."

I remember holding on to that sliver of light, milking it for comfort against terror that lurked behind closed eyes. The earliest dreams I can remember are from when I was maybe three or four. Witches flew above me through black skies; my own screams would wake me up. By elementary school, I dreamed of fire in the clothing store my grandparents had built below my room. Night after night, I dangled an arm from the bed, pressing a palm against thin carpeting, feeling for warmth. When I could not convince myself that the warmth I felt was just my own, I pulled aside the curtains and looked out at late-night dog walkers under streetlights, telling myself that if there really were a fire, those passersby would be staring and pointing at the store's window front. In summer, I left the window open a crack to reassure my racing heart with the sounds of unhurried feet and claws on paving stones.

In my mid-teens, I dreamed of running up and down stairwells I didn't recognize—not carpeted like those at home, but stone or concrete, bare, pitch-dark. The rooms in which I ended up had lost their roof and at least one of their outside walls. I'd awaken from my own shrieks as I stumbled and fell off the edge into the dark below.

When Oma Lotte told me about her dreams, I was eleven, maybe twelve. I was probably knitting while she pitted plums for cake or jam—a gray Saturday afternoon of autumn rain, soft kitchen light, and sweet smells bubbling from the stove.

I listened, knit two, purled one, my eyes glued to the baby sock Sister Bernadine had inflicted upon thirty girls as a first needlework project at my Catholic boarding school. Sweaty fingers clenched around knitting needles, I failed to pause, look up, and ask, "And when was this?" or "How old were you then?" And so the doctor's prescription wafted by and settled into memory, attaching itself not to a date or circumstance but to the aroma of simmering damson plums.

Stories, like balls of yarn, have a way of unrolling and interweaving in the retelling. When Oma Lotte told me about the doctor's prescription, I didn't think to ask her what she dreamed about when the dreams of knitting stopped. I didn't think to ask her why, as long as I could remember, a bottle of Adumbran sat on her bedside table, next to a glass of water and a book.

When Oma Lotte was in her seventies and I was in my teens, my family's naturopathic doctor, leery of pharmaceuticals, told me he couldn't bring himself to warn her that the bedside pills were bad for her. I've only recently looked up how bad: Adumbran is a benzodiazepine, an antianxiety drug that helps people sleep through the night. You're not supposed to take it if your heart is weak. You're definitely not supposed to take it if you're elderly. And you're most definitely not supposed to take it for more than two weeks. My Oma Lotte, with her weak heart, had been taking Adumbran for nearly twenty years—as long as it was on the market, as long as I had been alive.

In 1988, forty-three years after the end of the war, the German news magazine *Der Spiegel* reported that up to

25 percent of Germans over the age of sixty-five—the generation of wartime parents—took benzodiazepines or barbiturates. The article also reports that doctors prescribed tranquilizers for women twice as often as for men. The author goes on to speculate that doctors diagnosed female patients with "psychosomatosis" based on symptoms presumed physical in males.

Perhaps doctors' refusal to recognize anxiety as the likely cause of sleeplessness and heart palpitations in men explains the gender discrepancy in the prescription of sleeping pills. But it's also worth noting that some soldiers on family visits from the front described their experience in the bomb cellars as more frightening than anything they had lived through on the battlefield.

I do not mean to reduce the problem of tranquilizer dependency to a consequence of trauma suffered during World War II. But I believe that after the war ended, German doctors, themselves likely entangled in a web of wartime guilt and grief, were unprepared to treat—or even recognize—symptoms of post-traumatic stress. Four years before the war began, in 1935, all German doctors' organizations became *gleichgeschaltet*—politically aligned—under the leadership of the Nationalsozialistische Deutsche Ärztebund, whose members immediately passed regulations to remove Jewish doctors from the profession. Over the next decade, German doctors participated in forced sterilizations of 350,000 people and sent at least another 70,273 people with disabilities to their deaths. Doctors experimented on disabled children and adults, on political prisoners, and on people in concentration camps.

By the end of the war, 50 to 65 percent of German doctors had joined the Nazi Party. After the war, they largely refused to acknowledge any wrongdoing. Hans-Joachim Sewering, who reported at least nine of his disabled patients to the Nazi authorities, of whom at least five were killed, served as president of the German Medical Association until 1978. His obituary, written in 2010 by the then-president of the German Medical Association, omitted any mention of Sewering's Nazi past. What were the chances that the doctors governed by this medical association had let go of the Nazi idea that wartime traumas did not exist?

But subsequent generations of postwar doctors also failed to understand PTSD. A 2005 article in *Deutsches Ärzteblatt*, a professional journal for family physicians in Germany, stated that 27 percent of people over sixty-five—the generation of wartime children—suffered from emotional distress, yet doctors prescribed psychotherapy for less than one percent of them. "Dust, noise, shock, mortal fear, blast wave, shaking building, burning street, the sight of death and dying—all of this left behind emotional wrecks," Jörg Friedrich writes in *The Fire*, "people as ruined as their homes."

I think of the Valium the family doctor prescribed for my mother when, at maybe one year old, I refused to eat and he diagnosed her as "too nervous" to care for me. How, after a few weeks of taking it, she collapsed in the bathroom, couldn't get out of bed for a whole day due to profound dizzy spells, and threw away the pills. Her sister Elfriede's medications make her sluggish, heavy, dull. Each time Elfriede stops taking them, she is eventually sent to a psychiatric hospital. To my knowledge, no doctor has asked my mother or my aunt about their childhood experiences of the war.

In Germany, the idea that war can permanently sicken survivors arose when soldiers returned from World War I. The *Zitterer*, German for "tremblers," were so frequent among veterans that a connection between their experience in the trenches and their persistent, debilitating symptoms was undeniable: Many starved to death in understaffed hospitals because they shook too hard to feed themselves. American and British doctors called these soldiers "shell-shocked," and theorized that their brains were injured by the pressure waves set off by detonations. The French called them *invalides du courage* and honored them like other injured veterans. But German doctors constructed maps of symptom frequencies to demonstrate that the shaking was caused by an infection, supposedly transmitted by letters from home and by women during furloughs from the front. As treatment, they ordered either dunkings in ice water or electroshocks. Within a year of its rise to power, the Nazi government passed a law that denied all connections between war and psychological disability. Medical professionals eventually euthanized between four and five thousand trembling veterans of WWI.

"Tremors were a response to the bombed-out ground, which was no longer a firm base that a mobile person moved about on," Jörg Friedrich writes. "The energy from the munitions that was pumped into the earth in excess and converted into blast waves and radiant heat set the surroundings in motion. That was why all the descriptions included the image of the world going down: It was truly active, moving, vibrating, shaking, trembling, breaking, piling up, boiling, melting, falling to ashes. The firmness of the earth's crust makes us feel sure of a continuity. At the end of time, the crust breaks."

"Your Oma Lotte said she took me and Elfriede down to Southern Germany because the doctor said she should," my mother explains when I ask her why they left Essen with the very first evacuees, far ahead of the mass flight from cities that followed later. "I was shaking all the time."

My mother was barely a year old when Essen experienced its first major bombing raids. She was only four months old when the Nazis rolled out Aktion T4, the program under which doctors systematically euthanized people with psychological and physical disabilities. They began with the children.

Other families doused trembling toddlers with cold water, desperate to make them stop. I breathe a prayer of thanks to the doctor who pitted empathy and common sense against the mandated medical practices of his time.

"How is Elfriede?" I ask my mother on the phone.

"She hasn't been picking up her phone," my mother says. "I'll call the hospital tomorrow to see if she is there. Dad's watching soccer, do you want to talk to him?"

"In a minute," I say. "Are you sleeping okay?"

"I'm fine," my mother says. "The melatonin doesn't work, but the doctor says I can keep taking Gittalun. I try not to take more than a quarter pill and only when I'm not asleep by one or two a.m. Do you think that's okay?"

I punch "Gittalun" into Google, then pull up an article from the NIH's National Library of Medicine. Gittalun contains doxylamine, a first-generation antihistamine. The American Academy of Sleep Medicine recommends against using it to treat insomnia. It's not addictive, but in high doses it can cause drowsiness, dry mouth, hallucinations, or psychotic episodes.

I wonder how often my mother turns on her bedside lamp, fills a glass at the kitchen sink, and watches a fragment of an effervescent pill fizz to the surface and dissolve as her feet cool on the tiles.

"Yes," I say, pulling my finger away from the crack in the surface of my desk. A bead of blood forms where a splinter pierced my skin. "Yes, I think that sounds okay."

***Störkörper*, n. m.**

Ordinary metal detectors, the kinds that men swing back and forth along river edges in my Pennsylvania town, sense metals ten or fifteen inches below the ground. Bombs, falling from airplanes, can bury themselves six or seven yards deep. To detect their iron casings, you need a magnetometer probe. It looks like a yard-long, hollow, metal tube dangling from a rod. The rod connects the tube to a box of electronics you carry in your hands. The entire setup weighs about eight pounds.

Objects that set off a magnetometer but aren't really bombs are called Störkörper: "disturbing bodies." Sometimes there is no bomb. Sometimes there is no way to know whether the bomb is there but you haven't found it yet. This means that you must dig up each Störkörper, remove it, then walk, again, over the piece of ground you've just dug up because the coiled barbed wire, the old fire extinguisher, or the cans of rusty nails you've just unearthed might have hidden the bomb beneath.

NO ONE HAS IMAGINED US

A FAINT NOISE, AT FIRST, beneath my feet on the passenger side of the car. Balsam fir trees swish by the window in a blue-green blur. I glance at the steely expanse of the reservoir we pass, at the carless highway rolling on ahead. The closest town is twelve miles away. Not a great place to break down. I try to convince myself the wobble is uneven pavement. I try to tell myself the rumble isn't getting louder.

I finally ask Meg, who is driving, if she hears it too. She does. She slows, then speeds back up. The noise, the bumpiness beneath my feet, slows, speeds with the wheels. We're tourists here on New York State's Tug Hill Plateau, a day's drive from my home in northwestern Pennsylvania. Meg has flown in from Germany, where we both grew up, to talk by woods and lakes, to nurture a college friendship kindled thirty-five years ago. Now we both listen, our talk swallowed by grumbling running gear. A mile or so later, Meg pulls into a parking lot, marked as a trailhead to the Salmon River. Wobble or no wobble, Lena, my old dog, needs a stroll.

We inspect tires, pick small rocks from between treads.

Nothing looks wrong. I follow Meg around a rusted gate onto a gravel road and into the woods. Being with her grounds me. It always has. She started working as a geriatric care nurse soon after we met, and I understand why patients calm and settle in her care.

Where the road ends, at a collapsed bridge, we follow Lena's lead along a fisherman's trail through red osier and multiflora rose, down to the riverbed. Meg pokes at fish bones arranged on rocks, snaps pictures of a salmon's toothy skull. She's vegan, runs a rural animal rescue in her spare time, but she appreciates the elegance of this bony window into a life lived in deep current, the predator skinned into prey.

I watch Meg prod at stones and bones, try not to think of the fact that fishermen far outnumber fisherwomen in remote areas like this. Our quest for blue-green solitude has taken us where settlers nearly a century ago used to cut winter doors into the second floor of their cabins so as not to be trapped by Lake Ontario's snows. We're on plowed land where those early farms failed, now reclaimed by yellow poplar, maple, fir. We stand and listen as water rushes past orphaned bridge supports, skirt poison ivy on the way back to the parking lot.

The noise returns as we accelerate on the highway.

"Sometimes it's a CV joint," Meg says, "or a bad ball bearing. They get louder over time, but you can drive quite a way on those."

I think of the three hundred miles that separate us from my Pennsylvania town. It's Saturday; any car-repair shop is bound to be closed. Then again, the best day for two women to be stranded along a rural road with spotty cellphone coverage is never. Maggie Smith's poem "Good Bones" keeps playing in my head: "Life is short and the world / is at least half terrible, and for every kind / stranger there is one who would break you . . ."

I try to convince myself that Meg is right about bad ball bearings. But the sound is different than it was when I had them replaced two or three years ago. The front ones went first, then the rear. Either way, it started on turns, not on the straight. And it increased slowly, over many miles. This rumble is growing louder.

An hour later, the AAA tow truck driver scoots under the car on his back. Nothing looks wrong. The closest approved repair shop is an hour away. He would have driven us back to our cabin afterward, he says, but he's just returned from Afghanistan, can't risk losing his job. Instead, he lets me use his cell signal to download Uber onto my phone. When he sees my horror at the idea of leaving Lena to panic alone in my Prius as he maneuvers it onto his truck, he pats her head through the window and agrees to have her sixty pounds squeeze inside the truck's cab for the ride to the repair shop. We pass by a dozen Trump signs. The driver tells us about his own black Lab waiting at home, honks as we pass a roadside diner. "My sister works there," he beams. If Maggie Smith is right about fifty percent of the world, we're riding with the other half.

At the garage, all three of us look for a key-drop. The tow truck driver finally fishes a piece of notebook paper from his glove compartment, tells me to write my name and phone number on it, wrap it around the key, and push it into what he suspects to be the repair shop's mail slot. It feels like writing to Santa.

When the Uber driver arrives, she spreads a blanket on her back seat for Lena, then drives us by a dozen other Trump signs on the hour's drive back to our cabin. While she tells us her husband drives for Uber or Lyft too because it pays more than he made machining, that she has a second job working as a teacher's support, I wonder who they voted for, a nasty habit I picked up during the election twenty months ago. *If you knew that I'm an immigrant, would you vote me off the island?* I don't ask. I want her warm smile to mean she doesn't care where I was born, or whether I am gay or straight.

As we wait out the rest of the day in the sweltering heat, we wonder how we're going to get back to the repair shop. Lena solves the problem before we do by making friends with a border collie and a poodle staying in the cabin next door. Their owners, two women who have driven across three states in pursuit of their first pregnancy, are relaxing in the woods between doctors' appointments in Rochester. One of them, queasy with injected hormones, says she's happy to stay in the cabin while her wife drives us and Lena back to the repair shop—a three-hour commitment. She nearly refuses the gas money I press into her hand.

The repair shop owner is all smiles. He tilts his head, then squints as he slides paperwork toward me for a signature.

"Have you had work done on your wheels recently?"

I shake my head.

"Better talk to your repair shop at home about this."

He tells me that the left front wheel was about to come off. His mechanics retightened the lug nuts on three wheels—they all were loose. He says we were lucky we pulled over when we did, lucky it didn't happen on the interstate. I do feel lucky as I push two twenties across his desk.

"Could the nuts have worked themselves loose over time?"

"Nah," he says. "Those things don't come loose on their own. Someone forgot to tighten them right when they last rotated your wheels."

I shake my head again. My car dealer's shop has been in business for two or three generations. I bought the car from them, have had it serviced there for thirteen years, never had an issue.

On the drive home, Meg and I consider other possibilities. We parked next to the cabin, well off the highway, far away from the closest town or house. We would have noticed someone pulling up the long, curved gravel drive at night—motors cutting into silence, headlights slicing dark. Dogs would have barked.

Why would anyone want to unwrench the lug nuts on a Prius in the woods? No one knows us here. The lug nuts must have been loose before we arrived. Maybe it happened somewhere along the three hundred miles we drove to get here. But where? By the busy rest stop on the interstate? In a deserted parking lot at the Montezuma bird sanctuary, miles and miles from the nearest farm? Could they have been loose before we left my little town? Meg believes they could have been. She reminds me about the time someone partially unscrewed the lug nuts on her VW camper in Germany, thirty years ago. She drove that bus all the way through the hairpin turns of France's Massif Central before a wheel came off on the return trip along the autobahn, passing her as she slowed for a construction crew. She swerved between cones, stopped seconds ahead of a serious crash. At the time she suspected a psychotic neighbor of loosening the wheels before her trip to France.

Back home, I call my repair shop. Their records indicate they didn't touch my tires during my most recent service, last rotated them many months and thousands of miles ago. I decide to put the question out of my mind.

Six months later, I stare through December fog and darkness at the high waters of French Creek that gnaw the banks of my Pennsylvania town. My feet vibrate on the floor of my girlfriend's Subaru. She's driving us to the one restaurant in town that is warm and quiet enough for real conversation on a Friday night. My ears strain for the noise beneath my feet. I drag my attention back to Skye's voice. She's stressed, is barely hanging on between a more-than-full-time college teaching job and trying to be a good mom to her three-year-old. It's been a hard semester for both of us, a hard year for anyone supporting students who feel threatened in rural Pennsylvania.

Twenty-five months postelection, Trump signs still dot lawns and roadside ditches like flags planted across a game of *Minesweeper*. Anxiety and dread run under daily conversations, tugging at attention like noisy running gear. Comments in the local paper's anonymous "Sound Off" column have grown vicious toward college-educated people, non-Christians, immigrants, people of color, queers. A week ago, a man gunned down eleven men and women in a Pittsburgh synagogue an hour and a half away, close to many of our students' homes. On campus, swastikas have appeared on bathroom stalls, racial slurs on the doors of Black students' dormitory rooms. It feels as though we're sitting in a heating lobster pot. My biologist side has always known that we are getting boiled. The heat is rising much faster for some of us.

This evening is supposed to be our date night, a rare treat. We both need the break—a moment to breathe and talk while someone else cooks us a meal. I don't want my nerves to taint our time. Maybe the grinding rumble is normal for Skye's station wagon? But I've ridden with her enough to know that can't be true.

Uneven pavement, then.

"Do you hear that noise?" I blurt.

"Yes," she says, her voice tight. "I'm trying not to worry about it right now. I'll take the car in as soon as I can. Definitely before the Christmas road trip, though I don't know how to make that work."

Her tone warns me to lay off. The pit in my stomach wants to make her pull over immediately. I try to focus on what she tells me, try to forget the noise. I tell myself it isn't really getting louder. Bad wheel bearings, perhaps—there must be two dozen reasons for a car to vibrate and rumble in this way.

Two weeks later, I'm with family in Germany for Christmas, across the ocean, three thousand miles away. I scan Skye's face on my cellphone's screen. It's past midnight here, and I feel grateful for this long-distance window into her darkening room, even if the image and audio connection freeze from time to time. Her face is framed by the soft upholstery of her son's story-reading chair; the table lamp's light paints gold across her skin. Shadows under her eyes. She's scrambling to make it through meetings, grading, exams, departure preparations, gift-wrapping for her little boy. She still hasn't had a good night's sleep.

"And did I tell you about the car?" she says.

I shake my head, slowly, hoping her screen won't freeze the motion.

"It got so loud I didn't think it would make it all the way to the dealer's shop. But the people at the tire store just down the road have been really nice."

"Bad tire?" I ask.

She shakes her head. "Loose lug nuts on the back left wheel. They said it was about to come off. They asked me if I had it repaired recently, but the folks there only did things with the clutch last time. I called them to check."

The pit in my stomach bores down, rips open wide. "That's what happened to Meg and me, back in June. Three loose wheels and no work done recently."

"No way," Skye says.

We stare at each other. Our houses are a three-minute walk from each other, just around the block.

"That's spooky," she finally says.

When I still can't sleep, two hours later, I google news sites for "lug nuts," then mark reports on a computer map. Over the past several months someone has loosened wheels on police vehicles in Kentucky and on seemingly random private cars in Maryland, Virginia, Ohio, and Eastern Pennsylvania. Not exactly a cluster or a pattern.

When I tell my German friends about Skye's car, Meg's wife immediately asks if we've got a lesbian-hater in our neighborhood. I mentally scan houses, faces. I try to airbrush out the Trump signs.

Skye asks around: One neighbor also thought her car might have been tampered with a while ago. Another advises Skye to park her car in the garage. Maybe that's it—my garage has a dilapidated floor that makes it unusable. Hers is full up with her son's balance bike, stroller, scooter, little red wagon, kiddie pool, and plastic slide. Maybe we are the only ones who regularly park outside. Maybe I don't have to think of Adrienne Rich's line, *Two women sleeping / together have more than their sleep to defend.*

Maybe it's not the Trump signs, not someone resenting two women swinging a three-year-old boy, "one-two-three-*jump*," between their outstretched arms. Maybe it's not someone tracking who walks into whose house, sits in pj's on whose porch, parks in whose driveway and for how long. Maybe it isn't *Focus on the Family* blasting from the radios. Maybe it's just random mischief, a bored kid with a socket wrench and two cars sitting out on concrete in the early northern dark. Or maybe I should remember that a few weeks after Meg's wheel rolled past the window of her VW bus on the autobahn, her brakes were cut.

Sold, **n. m.**

In German, a soldier's pay is *Sold*. *Sold* is specific: it is only paid to soldiers. It is not "salary," which would be *Lohn*—a word that also means "reward."

Because the German word for "selling," *verkaufen*, bears no resemblance to *Soldat*, I never noticed the connection between them until the English past participle of "to sell" made it plain. Both the German *Soldat* and the English "soldier" derive from Latin *soldis*, meaning "money." *Soldat* did not originate to describe a man rewarded for heroic patriotic service. It meant a human body bought and sold.

STAR DOLLARS

IN THE EARLY SPRING OF 1943, Elfriede is five, Anna is three. Lotte is telling stories to keep the girls from crying as detonations shake the ground. Around them, the neighbors are singing: first Nazi propaganda songs, then, as explosions come closer and closer, switching to prayer and to hymns. Children scream. Lotte has wrapped Elfriede, Anna, and herself into a blanket. Sometimes dust and pieces of plaster fall onto the blanket from the basement ceiling. She pulls the blanket over their heads, like a tent, and rocks the girls on her lap, her mouth close to their ears: "Once upon a time," she begins, resorting again to Grimm's fairy tales, "there was a little girl whose mother and father had died . . ."

They had been evacuated to a farm in Southern Germany for a year, but now they're back in Essen and the bomb attacks have grown worse—more frequent, more destructive, relentless. Sometimes they run down to the basement three times in a single day. Often, they stumble down at night. Sometimes there are no explosions. Sometimes they are only in the distance. Sometimes they come very close. Lotte is good at inventing her own stories. But when she is overtired and afraid, she lets her mind roll down the familiar grooves of the stories she grew up with. Grimm's fairy tale "Sterntaler" is a story Anna and Elfriede have heard many times. In it, a little girl loses her parents and wanders off into the world. Already destitute, she gives away her last piece of bread, her little shirt, little skirt, and finally her underwear to people she perceives as worse off than herself. Eventually, God rewards her selflessness by turning stars into coins—"star dollars"—raining them down to her, and she becomes "rich all the days of her life."

One morning in early March of 1943, they climb up from the basement into devastation: blown-in windows, broken dishes. Lotte stands in the doorframe to her kitchen, her mouth tight, plump little Anna held on her hip with one arm, her other hand still clamped around Elfriede's wrist. "Stand right there," she says to Elfriede, letting go of her wrist. "Don't you move."

Lotte steps forward, crunch, crunch, across shattered glass and pottery, sweeps two broken plates and fragments of cups down from the kitchen counter with her free left arm, her sleeve pulled down around her fingers to protect her skin. The shards hit more shards on the linoleum. Tiny blue violets blink from fragmented porcelain around her feet. She plops wide-eyed Anna onto the counter, detaches Anna's fingers from her dress.

"Stay there, don't move!"

Crunch, one more step to the faucet. Twist. No water. Somewhere out there, a high-explosive bomb has hit a water main. Lotte grabs the broom, looks at her two wide-eyed girls. She takes a breath, begins to sweep, launching right back into the fairy tale: . . . *and the little girl was so poor that she no longer had a little room to live in, nor a little bed to sleep in . . .*

Lotte packs two suitcases. They are not very big. She is short. And pregnant. There's only so much she can lift. She tells the girls to hold onto her skirt as they pick their way through rubble to the railroad station. In a press of bodies, they're swept onto a train, and Lotte, magically, finds a seat. Someone lifts Anna and Elfriede into the baggage net above their mother's head. Other children stand on suitcases, wedged upright between adults. The train is out of standing room, the press of bodies around them too tight for anyone to fall as the wheels begin to roll. They roll and stop, roll and stop.

"Mom! Wake up! Mom! We're there!"

Each time Lotte drifts off to sleep, Anna yells from above Lotte's head. Lotte looks up at Anna's and Elfriede's eyes, huge above her, like four moons. She knows they know the story well enough, that, despite the train's rat-tat-tat, they will read her lips: . . . *and at last she had nothing else but the clothes she was wearing and a little piece of bread in her hand . . .*

Many hours later, the train stops for good, in Stuttgart. Lotte climbs out, someone hands down her two suitcases, her two small girls. She parks them at a table by the station's cafe, orders milk for the girls, a cup of coffee—there's coffee here!—for herself. She'll need the coffee to come up with a plan, an idea of where to go. Unlike their last escape to Southern Germany, this time they don't have a lodging assignment. The farm near Vogelsberg, where they stayed before, is nowhere close to Stuttgart. And it's probably filled with other evacuees.

Lotte blows on her coffee, but before she can take a sip, a hand grips her shoulder; the soldier shakes her, yells at her: "Get up, get up! You have to take the next train out, no matter where it goes! There's bombers flying in." He shakes her shoulder again. "Get up! Get out!"

Everyone is running. Lotte and the girls, holding fast to her skirt, are swept onto a platform, along the length of a waiting train, until, from the squeeze of bodies, from the mass of them, Elfriede and Anna are lifted, tossed through a window onto the train. They scream. Lotte screams too and then feels herself lifted, shoved after her little girls through the window, onto the overflowing train, the train that has already begun to move, and there are the soldiers who were lifting her, and there are her suitcases, in their hands, and here they come, in through the window, as the soldiers drop back and the train chugs out of the station hall.

When this train stops, they are in Ravensburg. Lotte has never been here before. She knows no one. Dazed, she wanders from the station, the suitcases too heavy, the girls much too tired now to walk. The porter at a hotel takes pity on her, turns someone else away. All cities with functioning hotels are awash in evacuees. Wartime rules say no one can stay in a hotel room for more than one week. Lotte unpacks her suitcases, finds nightgowns for the girls and for herself. They sleep.

The next morning, or the next, or the next, she must find a place for them to live. Down the road, there is a nursery school run by Franciscan nuns. Lotte grew up Protestant but married a Catholic, which meant she had to agree to raise her girls Catholic to avoid Alfred being excommunicated. It hadn't seemed to matter then; Essen's community of urban steelworkers had come to the Ruhr industrial area from many cultures. But now she's deep in Catholic southern Germany. Lotte answers honestly when the nuns ask whether she's Catholic and they raise their eyebrows, but they agree to watch the girls while Lotte scours the city for a place where they might live.

Nursery school in Ravensburg, to the girls, looks like a medieval fairy tale: The city's famous White Tower looms at the end of the street. Imposing women in black habits and blinding white coifs glide through tall, stony rooms. Here is one of them now, gathering her black skirt as she settles on a chair, surrounded by gray-faced children on the floor. She looks over her charges. Half of them, maybe more, have lost their homes. Many of them are thin, so thin. Many have lost their father, or their mother. Some lost both. The Lord will have to provide for them.

The black-robed sister puts a finger to her lips, *shhhhhh, shhhhhhh,* then opens a thick copy of *Grimms' Fairy Tales*: . . . *The little girl who had lost her mother and her father was good and pious, however. And as she was thus forsaken by all the world, she went forth into the country, trusting in dear God . . .*

At the end of "Sterntaler," when God rewards the pious little girl by raining coins from heaven, he also supplies her with a fine new shift with which to cover herself and to collect the "star dollars" in.

"Sterntaler" is the perfect Catholic allegory: The girl's poverty is akin to a nun's vow; her charitable renunciation of all her worldly goods purifies her soul until she is naked before God. The new shirt God bestows upon her at the end is a kind of christening gown, into which she collects the riches of heaven. Of course she is the heroine of Catholic story-time.

Lotte, meanwhile, knocks on doors. Over and over she is stunned to discover how few families here in this southern city, where no bombs have fallen, have volunteered to take in evacuees. When someone opens a door to her, she has a hard time understanding what they say.

"Sorry, I don't speak Schwäbisch," Lotte admits, then watches foreheads wrinkle, eyes grow small and hard, as women shape their lips and brains around the harsher sounds of High German to tell her there is no room.

No one seems able to imagine what has happened to her, or to the other women on the train, or to her city, how hard it is to stand here, asking for a room to rent. Sometimes she has to gesture, urgently, to tell them she needs a bathroom. It is a bad time to throw up from the kind of morning sickness that doesn't seem to care that it's already noon. When it happens, she knows there's no chance they'll say she can stay. A pregnant woman with two small kids? Sorry, this room you heard about is already taken. The nuns sent you? Are you Catholic then? No? Oh, so sorry, we don't actually have a room.

Lotte looks farther and farther afield but there is nothing, nothing at all. And now it's Sunday, and her week in the hotel is up. She's heard a rumor that a Protestant pastor in nearby

Schussenried takes in refugees. Most likely, she'll find him holding services in the library of the abbey there. Lotte dresses herself and her two girls in their nicest clothes, attaches them to her skirt, grabs her two suitcases, and gets on the train.

The abbey has its own stop. Lotte leaves her suitcases with the attendant, who tells her that Schussenried's small Protestant congregation has been using the abbey's famous baroque library for Sunday services for a hundred years; it even has a pipe organ. She follows the attendant's instructions, pulling her girls through the abbey's expansive grounds, first along the side of the church with its golden steeple, then up the external stairs to the entrance door of a tall, white building.

Partway up, the girls drag on Lotte's hands. She glances up as she, too, hears voices from above. Above the stairs, faces press against bars across an upstairs window, calling out, mouths big, eyes rolling, eyes wide. Arms wave through the bars. One of the arms dangles a doll toward the girls. The doll is made from dirty rags. The railroad attendant has neglected to tell Lotte that the Royal Asylum Schussenried took over most of the monastery grounds seventy years ago, including parts of the same building that houses the library. The voices from behind the barred window beckon to the little girls. Lotte speeds up, tugging Anna and Elfriede up the stairs—Anna nearly falls, unable to detach her eyes from the dangling doll—and then they are inside, their footsteps loud on ornate, polished tile, and there, at the end of the hall, tall wooden doors stand open, and when they pass through them, the ceiling just sweeps up and up.

Everything in this library gleams white, turquoise, and gold. The polished floor is a mosaic of white marble stars. Between turquoise marble columns, life-sized white marble figures in flowing marble robes pose on pedestals, holding golden staffs. Behind the statues, the walls are lined with books with gold-lettered leather spines. Above them, white cherubs seem to float around in air.

Elfriede stands and stares, open-mouthed, head tilted far back. Between the cherubs, gold-leaf-covered stucco frames a giant fresco on the ceiling. Figures in blue and red robes crowd its margins, and above them the ceiling swoops yet further up, covered in blue and white clouds among which more cherubs fly.

Lotte tugs on Elfriede's wrist. "Elfriede, say *Guten Tag* to Herr Pastor!"

Elfriede's head snaps forward; her mouth clamps shut. She curtsies to the man in the black suit.

The pastor agrees to let Lotte and her two little girls stay in his parsonage. It's clear that they can't remain there long, that they must vacate their room for others in need. But, for a few days, for a week, maybe two, they have a place, a bed.

By the end of March, the pastor finds a landlady in nearby Biberach who agrees to let Lotte and the girls share a room in her house with another evacuee who also has two children. Despite the cramped quarters, Lotte and her new roommate become fast friends.

The children, too, have playmates now, an entire gang of them: the roommate's two children, landlady Mrs. Klopp's four or five—far too many small, rambunctious bodies to tolerate inside the house. They are sent outside to play in the yard. At one end of the lawn, there are apple trees. The only instructions they are given for how to play are: one, don't get your clothes dirty, and two, if a plane swoops low, hurry up and dive under the trees. There haven't been bombers here, and probably there won't be, so far from industry. But the women know that fighter jets will strafe anything that moves.

Mrs. Klopp scolds and spanks the children for mud on their clothes. But as she does this, she stands them naked, one by one, in her kitchen sink to sponge them down. Lotte and her roommate exchange glances as they grab towels, ready to rub down clean, crying children. They know the spankings are not fair, especially not when they occur because the children dove under the trees when they heard the planes. But what are the mothers to do? They know they are out of options, can't antagonize the only woman who would take them in. Keeping this many children clean, the laundry washed, with running water only from the kitchen's tap, is near impossible as it is.

Lotte finds another nursing school to get the girls out of the house, at least for part of the day. More nursing school means more nuns, more Catholic story-time. Besides "Sterntaler," Elfriede and Anna hear tale after tale about damnation, eternal fires, the tortures of hell. The stories frighten them.

"But why do people go to hell?" Elfriede asks.

"Because they are Protestants," say the nuns. "Protestants go to hell."

"Protestants—like Mom?"

"All Protestants, dear child. So, yes, your mom. And also any Catholic little girl who sets even one foot inside a Protestant church."

Elfriede turns pale. She starts to cry.

When she comes home, Elfriede is still sobbing, her wet face pinched, snot running from her nose.

Lotte tries to comfort her, to hug her, but Elfriede shrinks back as though burned. "You're making us go to hell!" Elfriede screams. "We'll have to burn and it's your fault!"

She cries and cries, inconsolable. When Lotte finally understands that their visit to the pastor in Schussenried, the heavenly library of marble cherubs and painted saints, their days spent at the pastor's house, are what's causing Elfriede's rage and fear, Lotte tries to reason with her, but she fails.

Desperate, Lotte writes to Alfred to ask him what to do. She does not hear back. She has not had a single letter from him since they arrived in Biberach. Lotte tells herself that Alfred is writing to her, probably almost every day, but that he likely has not yet received her new address. Perhaps his letters are piling up in a post office in Essen, where bombs are still falling regularly; it may not yet be clear where the post office should forward them. Lotte has sent her relatives her new address, now that she has a place to stay, but for her letter to get to Essen, for someone there to tell the post office, or to go pick up her letters and send them here—a week, or two, or three may not be enough.

The girls' fear of nursing school, their tears, the perpetual nausea and fatigue, the horde of children in and out of the house, the tight space—it's all too much. Lotte flees. She takes

Elfriede and Anna to visit the farm in Vogelsberg, a day's train journey to the north, where they stayed when they were evacuated the first time. The brother and sister who run the farm had fallen in love with little Anna when they stayed there before, so Lotte knows they'll be welcomed for an Easter visit.

And yes, when they arrive in Vogelsberg, Herr Bullinger is still just as taken with Anna as he ever was, and Anna with him. She follows him everywhere. When Anna wets her pants, Herr Bullinger rinses them under the pump in the farmyard, then hangs them on a fence to dry. There are no harsh words. The two of them come in from the cowshed, from the pigsty, from the pasture, from the fields, and Anna is all smiles, her cheeks rosy. She seems more content than Lotte has seen her in many months. Elfriede remains uneasy, tight. But there are no more tantrums, no more tears.

Lotte knows that she can't overstay her welcome, but when she packs their bags to go, brother and sister implore her to leave Anna with them. Lotte hesitates. The last time, when she took the children back to Essen because they had to make space for new evacuees, Herr and Frau Bullinger begged her to leave Anna with them, to let them adopt her. They were too old to find spouses and have children, they argued. They needed an heir for their farm. Lotte was still young, they said. She could always have another child. Lotte had looked at them and just kept folding Anna's diapers, her little dresses, her socks. Their intensity scared her.

But now, for sure, they have understood that Anna is hers, not theirs. That leaving Anna with them will just be an extended visit, not an adoption. And they are right: bringing two children back with her to the little house in Biberach is too much. Lotte still can't keep food down. Her belly and legs swell more each day. Leaving Anna here will mean one less child for the landlady to scold and spank. Here, two doting adults will watch her, be patient with her. She'll have fresh air, kindness, and plenty to eat. And Anna says she wants to stay. Lotte gives in.

In Biberach, Elfriede is sent back to nursing school, back to the nuns, straight back to tales of hell: "Child, you stayed—where? With the *pastor*? The *Protestant* pastor? You went into his *church*?"

By June, Alfred's letters find Lotte, finally. He admonishes her for leaving Anna at the farm. "This can't be good," he writes. "You know how hard it was for Anna to leave last time, how hard it was for them to let her go. This will only make it worse. And as for Elfriede? Just keep her home! Don't let any nuns tell her some bullshit tales that make her all upset!"

But Lotte, by now, is not just six months pregnant but also supposed to stay in bed. Her last baby died inside her womb, right around the sixth month of pregnancy. How can she run after Elfriede all day long? Her roommate and the landlady are managing cooking, cleaning, washing, and grocery shopping for all the children by themselves. Asking them to watch Elfriede on top of that? She just can't.

Lotte doesn't have an answer to Alfred's questions about what will happen to the girls when she goes into labor. Each of her previous three births (the two girls and the stillborn baby) ended in a caesarean section. Each brought her close to death. She recovered slowly, slowly from each one. She has no clue where the children might stay when she is hospitalized this time.

Alfred, meanwhile, writes of mud, of units moved in haste, of interrupted mail. Letters, both ways, get lost or take weeks and weeks to arrive. It is the summer when Soviet troops begin to push Hitler's armies back. Death tolls skyrocket on both sides. All of Lotte and Alfred's friends and relatives are still in Essen, a place of hunger, of houses turned to rubble, of nightly bombing raids. Lotte and the children are on their own. They cannot go back home. Neither Alfred nor Lotte can think of where to send the girls, or where Lotte and the children might live once the baby has arrived.

And so Elfriede goes to Catholic nursing school, day after day. "Pray hard, child," say the nuns, "so that your sins may be forgiven, and you may be saved from hell." "Your mother is Protestant, so she can't be saved. All you can do is pray to save yourself." "Think of the little girl in 'Sterntaler,' how pious she was. How good." Elfriede thinks of the Sterntaler girl, how she gave her last piece of bread to the beggar, her cap to the child whose head was cold, her jacket to another freezing child, her dress to a third child, and finally, her shift to yet another child. She thinks of the little girl dancing, naked, under the tall sky as God rains the stars from heaven down on her.

After many admonishments from Alfred, Lotte will bring Anna home from Vogelsberg sometime around early June, and Anna, too, will go back to nursery school in Biberach. By mid-August, Lotte's health will deteriorate to the point that she is hurried off to the university hospital in Tübingen.

Lotte's landlady in Biberach will put Elfriede and Anna on a train, with cardboard signs around their necks. A driver will pick them up from the train station in Reinstetten and take them to an orphanage in Schönebürg that's run by Elizabethan nuns. For two months, Elfriede and Anna will be surrounded by orphaned children, while their mother fights to survive her fourth caesarean sixty miles away and their father is thousands of miles away in Russia, where the German front collapses and retreats.

"I only received your address today," the girls' father will write, in a letter that is dated two weeks after Elfriede's sixth birthday:

> By now, you have already been there for four weeks, and, hopefully, the time will soon be over so you can again be home with Mother. As Mother wrote to me, you have been good lately, when she was ill. I hope you will be especially good now that you are in the orphanage. When you receive these lines, it won't be very long before I will be on furlough. By then, Mother, too, will be healthy again. But I hope that Mother and I will not have to hear complaints about you.
>
> Hopefully, you are still healthy and cheerful, which I can also say about myself. Especially you, Elfriede, must be careful—and watch Anna carefully, to make sure she does not commit any follies. Though Anna now is already big and sensible, and, hopefully, always good.
>
> And if you pray with enough fervor every night, then Mother will soon be well again, and we can all meet at

> her house. Until then I send you many kisses and shall remain,
>
> Your Dad

Elfriede will pray, hard. Elfriede will be good.

Decades later, Elfriede will fixate on images of Satan as a regular feature of her manic episodes. Another persistent feature of her mania will be that she gives away everything she owns—by sending packages to friends and relatives, by handing her TV and radio and furniture to people in the street, and finally by taking off and giving away the clothes she's wearing. Over and over, police will take her to a psychiatric hospital for dancing naked in the streets. No God rains star dollars from heaven down on her—but perhaps, at times, her mania will make it feel as though he did.

The Nazis, too, loved the Sterntaler girl. In 1945, months before the end of the war, they reapproved screenings of a short "Sterntaler" film, listing the story as *volksbildend*, "educational for the people." The story's moral—impressing on young minds the virtues of sacrifice, resilience, and discipline in the face of hardships—lent itself not just to turning little girls into aspiring nuns, but also to shaping children into soldiers for the *Endsieg*.

Perhaps the beggar who got the Sterntaler girl's last piece of bread, the children who got her clothes, were saved by her gifts. Or perhaps the fairy tale Jakob Grimm collected and wrote down "from dark memory," as he put it, simply described what people saw in times of war: an abundance of heroic little girls who found seemingly miraculous ways to survive impossible circumstance.

At the time, Elfriede's ardent prayers, her "Sterntaler"-like piety, seemed to Lotte to be reasonable, necessary: an appropriate response to dire need and daily worry about survival. In the bomb cellars, everyone prayed, even people who had not set foot in a church in years. Prayer offered the only plan of action for children whose fathers were soldiers at the Russian front—the more Elfriede prayed, the better. Children, in my grandmother's mind, came equipped with a special telephone line that went straight to God. In southern Germany, far from home, the girls needed that direct connection to the top. If Elfriede wanted to pray a lot, that seemed like the best thing she could do.

Jakob Grimm wrote "Sterntaler" in 1810, somewhere near Kassel, in Hesse. His location likely inspired the story's title: three decades earlier, thousands of Hessian families had received silver coins stamped with stars. These "star dollars" were still in circulation when Grimm wrote the tale. They had been coined by Landgrave Friedrich II, who sold about 17,000 Hessian soldiers to Britain from 1776 to 1779. The British Crown, in desperate need of soldiers to stand against rebellious colonists in America, paid Friedrich II handsomely for these men. Some were press-ganged into service against their will. Others signed on to military service in desperation to save their families from abject poverty: Their contract stipulated that a soldier's dependents would be financially provided for if he should die.

In 1935 Germany, the conscription of men into Hitler's Wehrmacht wasn't much different. When Lotte finds out that she is pregnant, Alfred spends frantic weeks searching for a job in a collapsing economy, asking everyone he knows for help, for any leads at all. They cannot marry unless he has a way to pay for rent and food. The situation becomes so dire, Lotte's "Uncle" Norbert tells her that if Alfred can't find work before the baby arrives, then Norbert will marry her, to spare her from becoming an unwed mother with no support.

As sleepless weeks stretch into months, Alfred finally lands a desk job in a building cooperative called Eigene Tat. The name might loosely translate as "own deed" or "work of one's own hands." At a time when workers have no money for down payments on a home, the cooperative intends to build houses by investing their own manual labor: thousands of hours to build homes for each other. At first, the houses are simple single-family dwellings. By the time Alfred is hired, new members with some money to invest have joined, and the cooperative is now able to bring on office staff and can tackle larger projects such as apartment buildings. Alfred will be forever grateful to the man who runs the cooperative, the man who chooses to hire him so that he and Lotte can marry. To this day, the cookie-cutter houses and tenements built by Eigene Tat still determine the character of parts of Essen.

A photograph from that time shows Alfred framed by two other young men, all three of them absorbed in paperwork piled on the desk in front of them. The man to Alfred's right is holding a pen in the same hand that holds his chin as he ponders the paper on which Alfred is pointing to something with his own pen. The man to Alfred's left is speaking into a phone, receiver pressed to his ear. A pipe dangles from the corner of Alfred's mouth. I don't know who took this image, or why it was taken, but the scene it captures appears carefully staged to convey absorption into the shared, important work of men—urgency, purpose, togetherness—the values of a workers' movement that characterized the unionized laborers who lived and worked in close proximity. It is the kind of solidarity that the Nazis will soon seek to replace with ideological alignment and Party loyalty.

Three or so years after Alfred is hired, his boss will call the young men into his office. He will explain that he has held off a takeover of the cooperative by the Nazi government as long as he could. "Alignment" of the cooperative under new Nazi administrators will entail having the houses the workers have been building for each other instead assigned to Party operatives. The boss can see only one way to prevent the takeover: to signal that the cooperative already is "aligned," each of the men who work in the office will have to join a Nazi organization. To determine who will join which organization, they draw straws. The straws say "Party Membership," "SS," or Sturmartillerie, which means "assault artillery." Alfred draws Sturmartillerie. He must volunteer for a patriotic military organization that is stationed close to Essen.

Lotte is furious. Alfred tells her he has no choice. If they want to eat, to feed two-year-old Elfriede, baby Anna, and the child Lotte is yet again pregnant with, if they want to eventually own a home, he must go.

A few months later, Alfred's unit of the *Sturmartillerie* is whisked away to France. When Alfred's unit is called up again, this time to be sent east, toward what will become the Russian front, he runs home to tell Lotte they are leaving. He only has minutes to let her know—no time to plan or discuss anything, no time for a real goodbye. Still breathless, he hugs Lotte and runs back down the stairs. Lotte stands in the doorway of their apartment, holding on to the doorframe as blackness closes in behind her eyes. Behind her, baby Anna and Elfriede wail in their cribs. Inside her womb, Lotte feels baby number three stop moving. She will never feel it move again.

Some historians point out that Friedrich II did in fact take care of the widows and orphans of the fallen and disabled Hessian soldiers, and that his charitable foundations helped poor families well into the twentieth century. They say that loaning out or selling soldiers was just what was done at that time. They argue that this was how Friedrich financed modernizing Hesse's economy and industry. But I can't help thinking of the postcard-sized prints of historic lithographs my mother hung on the wall in our hallway at home: the expansive palace at Kassel Wilhelmshöhe, the fake-medieval Lion's Castle, the giant fountain, and the enormous artificial waterfalls—all part now of a UNESCO World Heritage Site preserving monumental baroque architecture. All constructed by Wilhelm IX—Friedrich's son. All paid for in blood. Soldiers' blood.

About 6,500 of the Hessian soldiers that were sold to the British Crown by Landgrave Friedrich II never returned. The "star dollars" he coined to pay them and their families were called "blood dollars" in America. They weren't rare when

Jakob Grimm penned "Sterntaler," and they aren't considered rare by collectors today.

Who, then, is Jakob Grimm's "Dear Lord," who rains down golden stars on an orphan girl? Is he a Catholic god? Or is he Friedrich II of Hesse Kassel, stamping stars onto silver to pay for deaths? And what happened to the Sterntaler girl's parents? Was her father killed in America? Did her mother die while giving birth?

Eighty or more years after the end of the war, an online boutique that sells plush toys, toddler clothes, and babyware in Germany takes the name Sterntaler. The fairy tale is still printed in children's books and made into German public television movies for children. You can buy "Sterntaler" picture cards, so-called "Romantasy" "Sterntaler" adaptations as books for teens, instructions for staging "Sterntaler" puppet plays and for crocheting your own "Sterntaler" dolls.

There is an illustration on page 326 of my half-century-old copy of *Märchen der Brüder Grimm*: A little girl stands, barefoot, under a star-studded sky. Her brand-new shift glows white as her small hands hold it open to catch the rain of coins.

> This girl, dear God, this girl in her white shift,
> she's standing in a rain of blood.
> I watch her blink the splatters from her lashes, lift her naked feet.
> Slowly, she begins to step, to turn, to twirl.
> She'll dance the blood back into stars.

Standardabweichung, n. f.

Standard deviation. Not an oxymoron. Not a joke. In the midst of a class discussion in 1986, my biology professor calls me "the standard deviator," supposedly because I take his enzyme kinetics class a year or two earlier than most. Or maybe because I am a girl who very much loves math.

Standard deviation is the square root of the variance, which quantifies how far measurements stray from an average. Consider that the statistics we still teach in colleges and universities sprang from eugenics: Sir Francis Galton's idea that "those afflicted by lunacy, feeble-mindedness, habitual criminality and pauperism" should be "discouraged" from having children. Consider how both *Abweichung* and deviation suggest the process of veering from a path: the German word with its root in the Proto-Indo-European **weyk-*, "to bend or to curve," the English from the Latin *de via*, "off the way." Consider that, since the seventeenth century, "to deviate" implied that you violated expectations someone in power set for you: you broke their rule of conduct, failed to satisfy their norms, went against their plan. Consider how "standard deviation" insists that we must seek to "standardize" such slithering departures from an average: to judge them according to where someone planted a flag. Consider that biology might be flagless: not a railroad track from which soft organisms deviate, but a wild dance on a globe that floods and heats and freezes, dries and cracks, a reckless rumba on tectonic plates that clash and bounce and spew gases and ashes, sulfur, hot magma. Consider how life's persistence in a changing world depends on dancing deviants.

PEAR SOUP

IT IS LATE AUGUST OF 1943. Elfriede and Anna are in Elisabethenpflege, an orphanage in Schönebürg, only ten miles from Biberach, where they and Lotte had lived with the stern landlady, and sixty miles from Tübingen, where their mother is now hospitalized at a Nazi-run "home for mothers" close to the university hospital while she waits on bed rest for the birth of their brother.

"But I am the older one," the smaller girl says. Her blue eyes flash defiance, curls radiate from her head. She holds her sister by the wrist. The chubby-cheeked girl by her side towers over her by nearly a full head, but her bottom lip is quivering.

Sister Sabina watches Sister Canysia take a second look at the birth dates in the girls' files, discreetly counting months on her fingers beneath the surface of her desk. Sabina doesn't blame her. It's hard to believe that Anna, the taller girl, is nearly twenty months younger than little Elfriede, whose sixth birthday is coming up next week.

The size reversal is so striking that, for a moment, Sabina

wonders if the two girls might have been playing games, exchanging the cardboard name signs hanging from their necks. But no: the driver, who delivered them here from the railroad station in Reinstetten, would have forbidden them to take off their signs. After years of war and delivering small children from railroad to orphanage, he knows that no child can be reunited with her parents unless strict tabs are kept on who is who. Before he met them on the platform, the girls must have been on the train for less than twenty minutes—it's just a few stops to Reinstetten from Biberach, where their mother's landlady had put them on. They look scared enough that Sabina can't imagine them getting bored with being alone on a train and planning some kind of nonsense.

In the weeks that follow, Sister Sabina never again doubts who is the older one. Elfriede doesn't let her sister out of her sight. No child taunts Anna without repercussions, no adult needs to check that Anna's teeth are brushed or that her hair is combed. On Sister Sabina's final round through the junior girls' makeshift dormitory in the attic, she has grown accustomed to finding Anna in Elfriede's bed, Elfriede's arms protectively around her younger sister, holding on, even in the depths of dreams.

Forty-three years later, my parents and I stand in a wood-paneled hall. We have walked through several locked doors to get here. The ceiling is tall, far above our heads. The nurse asks for our names before she leaves through another tall wooden door to fetch Elfriede.

I'm twenty years old, home from college for the weekend. When the call came this morning that Elfriede had been committed to a psychiatric hospital, my mother seemed to come unglued: unable to sit down, pacing between frantic phone calls. Even my father seemed shaken, unsure what to do. I couldn't imagine getting on the train back to school, couldn't imagine sitting in genetics class, wondering how my parents were holding up, wondering what they would find. Or whom: Elfriede, the competent nurse? Or Elfriede who glues photographs and magazine clippings all over her apartment walls, Elfriede who rages on the phone, calling her mother Satan incarnate?

"I've bought myself a little tiger," Elfriede says.

I feel my mother tighten next to me, watch the image flash through both our minds: a cub, striped fur, teeth, claws. How big? From where? A wild beast snatched from its parents, bound to grow enormous, all-devouring, a raging flame—

I search Elfriede's face, the sparks in her blue eyes beneath cropped, ash-blonde curls.

"At the gift shop?" my father asks.

My mother exhales. The gift shop. Stuffed.

Elfriede nods. She says she's doing well. Very well. So very well.

None of us mention that the police brought Elfriede here. None of us ask about the elderly man she was hired to nurse, and nursed so very well, for months. Has he recovered from Elfriede pushing him, in his wheelchair, through busy streets, to the busy plaza beneath Cologne's famous cathedral, at breakneck speed, singing, stopping here and there to take off pieces of her clothing, give them away? From watching her dance, naked, beneath the looming towers of the church?

We don't stay long. This is the only time I can remember visiting Elfriede in the hospital at Marienborn, though she will be brought here over and over again. For years, she will drift from long periods of extreme caretaking into hallucinatory manias. Usually, the police bring her to the hospital after she gives away all her possessions, ending with her clothes. Each time, the doctors release her when she calms down enough that they believe she might stay on her medications for a while. Each time, eventually, there is another phone call from a hospital, or from a landlady asking who's going to clean up the apartment, to pay for damage to the walls.

Sister Sabina catches a glimpse of Anna and Elfriede as she passes by the portal to the children's dining hall. Again, Elfriede is standing ramrod straight, her iron grip around Anna's pudgy wrist. Sabina can see her lips move as she turns to Anna's tear-streaked face: "We don't do that."

Sabina knows the words—repeated each time Anna is ready to join the other children in a folly, a small infraction. Now, as always, Elfriede is serious, unyielding. Sabina steps through the door, scans the dining hall. Elfriede must have just pulled her younger sister away from the other kids, who are spooning soup from the floor. The tall windows are open wide, admitting a warm breeze laced with the cloying aroma of overripe pears. Sun flecks dance across the new linoleum, the white walls. Anna stands next to Elfriede, watching the children with longing. The soup has been the first sweetness these children have had in many weeks. In the midst of this war, the Lord has blessed the orphanage's orchard with an abundance of late-ripening fruit—more pears than can fit into their supply of canning jars. More even than can be boiled down for thick pear juice, their only reliable supply of sugar.

The puddle of soup on the floor is nearly gone, and Sister Adela has not yet emerged from the kitchen to discover the damage. The older girls in charge of serving the midday dinner must have handled the entire calamity. Sabina feels pleased with them. In this time of lack, a small upset can have large consequences, but the older girls have kept their heads. Most likely, one of them stumbled when they carried the soup kettle from the kitchen. Or the kettle flipped when they tried to set it on a stool that is low enough for them to dip the ladle. They must have turned the kettle upright, then told all the girls to bring their spoons and eat the soup from the floor. They know the linoleum is spotless. Two of the girls mopped it this morning, after porridge was served for breakfast.

Adela steps from the kitchen, raises an eyebrow, then inquires with the two supervising girls, sends them for mops and buckets. She's preoccupied, has not noticed that Anna and Elfriede are standing by.

Sabina makes her way over to them. "You children should eat!"

Anna, spoon in hand, turns to join the others, but is brought up short as Elfriede's grip retightens on her wrist. The corners of Anna's mouth twist in protest as she turns back to her sister, but she says nothing. Sabina looks at

Elfriede's thin, pinched face, feels steel-blue eyes seeking her gaze straight-on.

"No," Elfriede says. "We don't do that."

"Don't do what?" Sabina asks.

"We don't eat from the floor."

Sabina considers arguing that the floor has just been cleaned, dismisses it as useless. Elfriede's standards of cleanliness far exceed those of any other child. She will starve before she will compromise. Adela, Sabina knows, will have none of this, will send them away without food. But Elfriede, slight and pale when she arrived, has grown painfully thin in the four weeks that have passed since then. Her cheeks are hollow. Depressions have deepened below her collarbones. The letter from the girls' father leaves no doubt that he will ask questions when he returns from Russia to retrieve his daughters—which may be months from now. Sabina glances at Adela's back, then calmly turns toward the sisters. "Come with me."

She walks the girls down the hallway, into the kitchen by way of the scullery. She takes two bowls from the long shelves lining the walls, ladles soup, places the bowls on the kitchen table. "Eat up quick," she tells the girls, "and then rejoin your group."

Perhaps two years after the hospital visit with the tiger, I stood about twenty miles from Elfriede's hospital at Marienborn, on a grassy farm track by a field of wheat. The field was very flat. It was very silver green. It smelled of summer and it smelled of wind. It smelled of blooming wheat, the semen-like ripeness of pollen on the wind. Just then, in May or early June, it had a sort of even smell—as though nothing could ever change in the cycle of ripeness and yield. The absence of insects and birds echoed in the swish of blade against blade, the hum of the greenhouse ventilators down the road, the cultivator five or six fields over, and in our silence between the words of our guide, a geneticist in jeans, button-down shirt, and sandals, worn with socks.

"This," he said, his hand pointing, "is the second generation after the cross. Notice how the plants are all different heights, how the awns have different lengths, the kernels different sizes." He crushed one wheat spike in his hand, then another, thumb grinding against palm. Unripe grains popped from glumes, revealing different plumpnesses, greennesses, grainnesses.

There should have been crickets. There should have been flies and the swallows' twit-a-twit as they swooped in circles, dove, shot up, beaks filled. Instead, only the hum of the cultivator, only the rustle of one student's nylon raincoat against another, the shifting weight from one foot to the next.

"This," the geneticist continued, scattering kernels and chaff, sweeping his arm toward the next neat block of plants, "is the fourth generation, this the sixth, eighth, and, finally, there's the tenth." The grass of the farm track slicked and squeaked under our sneakers as we spun. As our eyes followed his hand, the wheat plots became movie frames, a flip-book: The shaggy-dog look of the initial cross flattens out, morphs into crew cuts, the movie's final frame a battalion of elite soldiers, all of them even in bulk and height.

It was 1988. We were all white. We were in Köln Vogelsang, the field station of the Max Planck Institute for Plant Breeding Research. Yes, we had grown up alongside the children of Turkish "guest workers" in our elementary schools, but few of them had gone on to university, and none were on this particular multiday field trip for a class that was supposed to show us where people with biology degrees might work.

Was it me who asked why? Why breed for ten or twelve generations, a decade or more, to end up with this evenness? The answer was: machines. Run the combine harvester at one height. Sift uniform-sized grain away from dirt and rocks. Cut all plants on the same day, knowing each grain is ripe, holds identical, ideal moisture. Guarantee the mill, the bread factory, this much gluten, this much sweetness, starch, this stickiness, this stirrable-ness, this rise. Identical loaves, batch after batch, bag after bag.

It had been all around me growing up as I raced my bike up and down the road at my grandparents' house, through oat and potato fields, or later, as I rode horses through summer-scented wheat-wheat-wheat that had, for centuries, made my hometown's wealth. It had never occurred to me that the oats whose kernels released milky sweetness when crushed between my teeth, the wheat, the potatoes, the sugar beets that scented my town's air with molasses from the factory, could be shaggy, mosaics of different greens, different rustles, different scents. Köln Vogelsang was the place, the moment when I understood that wheat, like any crop, did not just come the way it was, all one hue, one size, one frame of ripe. That we had made it so.

When I search for official records of Elisabethenpflege online, I find an *Erlass*, a decree, by Württemberg's minister of the interior that passed into law on November 7, 1938. It spells out that all of Württemberg's orphaned children were to be classified into "the following groups":

I. Mentally and genetically healthy children
II. Physically handicapped children, including deaf and blind children, with normal mental capabilities
III. Children with genetic defects or signs of advanced neglect
IV. Children with severe mental handicaps or psychological pathologies
V. Gypsies and children that resemble gypsies.

I think of what happened to more than five thousand children classified as groups II, III, IV, or V all over Germany. When the Nazi Party came to power in 1933, it immediately passed the "Law for the Prevention of Offspring with Hereditary Diseases," which enabled the euthanasia program that was later named Aktion T4. By 1939, all doctors were required to submit questionnaires about patients whom they deemed "feeble of the mind" to Tiergartenstrasse 4, a house in Berlin. There, "expert" doctors hired by the extragovernmental "Kanzlei des Führers" labeled as *lebensunwert* (unworthy of life) anyone suffering from a disease deemed "heritable," such as schizophrenia, alcoholism, or dementia. They especially targeted patients who had been ill for a long time, were no longer able to work, and did not have relatives who checked on them frequently. The Ministry of the Interior then sent notes to the caregiving hospitals, asylums, or orphanages that these patients must be transferred to Schussenried or one of many other psychiatric hospitals that were used as "interim institutions" (*Zwischenanstalten*) for patients that had been selected to be sent to one of only six "killing hospitals" (*Tötungsanstalten*). Grafeneck alone drew its victims from a network of forty-eight Zwischenanstalten, each of which transported between two and five hundred patients to Grafeneck. A few months later, relatives of the patient would receive a note from these "interim" hospitals that their family member had, unfortunately, succumbed to a disease, usually pneumonia.

The program initially concentrated on children below the age of three, who were killed by injection of chemicals. With the beginning of the war, criteria for selecting patients for euthanasia were broadened, age limits rose rapidly, and gas chambers increased the number of patients who could be killed in one day. Eventually, as so many children began disappearing from institutions where they had been transferred to purportedly receive "improved treatment," parents grew suspicious. If parents refused to give up their disabled children, authorities would threaten to take their other children away and commit the parents to forced labor unless they complied. Families of adult patients also began to hear of disappearances; many tried to get their relatives released from psychiatric hospitals. In Baden-Württemberg, these Aktion T4 euthanasia programs were carried out through lethal injections in hospitals or through carbon monoxide gas in Grafeneck Castle, less than an hour's drive from Schönebürg.

Elisabethenpflege was assigned to accept only children in "Group III" of Baden-Württemberg's 1938 *Erlass*. But reality might well have been much more chaotic than official Nazi rules: over the course of the war, an estimated twenty million children in Germany lost one parent, half a million lost both—orphanages were flooded with children everywhere. Most likely, the landlady in Biberach simply sent Anna and Elfriede to Elisabethenpflege because it was the closest orphanage that had space.

When I ask my mother if she has heard from Elfriede, she says no. "Not this week, but sometime next week, I'll ask your father to look through the package that she sent four months ago."

My mother tells me she put Elfriede's package in the basement when it arrived. I can imagine where: top shelf, well toward the unlit end, away from the dim window, above eye level, by the boxes of winter boots and heavy binders of old tax returns awaiting the date after which they can be tossed. She doesn't want to see it when she ventures down for bottled water, for veggies from the chest freezer, for canned tomatoes or extra shopping bags.

"Last time I called, she sounded alright again," my mother says, "so now your dad can fish out any items that might still be useful to her and I'll mail them back. The rest he can put in the trash. I don't want to know about any of it."

I can guess what the still-useful things and "the rest" might be. Decades ago, Oma Lotte occasionally mentioned the things Elfriede would send her in packages like the one in my mother's basement now: a hand mixer, a hairbrush, toothpaste, shoe polish—household goods that, if you have to repurchase them every few months, add up for someone who lives on social security. "The rest": collages of images from catalogs and cut-up family photographs, bizarre junk sculptures, a long letter berating my mother for not caring for my father's early-stage dementia and mobility problems the right way. Make him drink holy water from the church's stoup, or cart him to a faith healer Elfriede has just discovered who can heal "anything!!!!" In between recipes for miracle healings, the letter will also threaten that ignoring Elfriede's advice will mean the devil has closed my mother's mind. There will be vivid descriptions of what Satan will do to my mother if she does not turn away from him. Most likely, there will be lengthy passages of "proof" that Lotte too was possessed by Satan (or, in fact, embodied him) when she was alive.

I can't blame my mother for not wanting to look.

Wild wheats are tall and short; green, gold, and red; ugly and beautiful; sickly and strong. Some plants will germinate and ripen early, some very late. Some grains will be full of the best kind of starch for bread, some will be small, low in gluten, a pain to sift and grind, unfit for fluffy, yeasted loaves.

To select against this diversity means to weaken the entire population, to lessen its chance of surviving the next catastrophe. This is why we keep seeds of wild and woolly wheats in doomsday vaults buried at the Arctic Circle deep in rock. This is why we must keep growing old and wildish wheats on farms, where they evolve with downpours, droughts, and wind, with locusts, rusts, and blights.

To grow all your wheat in just one way, to eliminate the ugly kernels, the late or early ones, is to kill your future. The plant with few, small kernels may be the one that resists drought, or insects, or disease. The plant that struggles and lags in too much rain may be the one with roots shallow or deep enough to find scarce nutrients.

All of her life, my mother has been unable to argue. Any tiny discord sends her heart into overdrive, turns her mind to cotton wool, shakes her knees. All of my life, my mother has begged me not to quarrel with my sister, because my mother's knees are shaking. My mother wants me to keep peace with my sister: peace, peace, peace. My mother says she doesn't want to hear what my sister has or hasn't done. She doesn't want to hear what I want or do not want. She says all that matters is that there is peace, peace, peace. She says there will never be peace in the world unless I make peace with my sister. My mother says all she ever wanted was to get to keep the older sister who protected her.

When I ask my mother what it was like, in the orphanage, her face closes down, the way it always does when conversations drift toward the war.

"Oh, it was hard," my mother says, and asks, immediately, if I would like more tea.

I shake my head no, willing her not to get up from the table, not to end this conversation.

She gathers cake plates, saucers, cups, then looks up. "But I always had my sister. She was watching out for me. I never felt alone." She pushes the stacked porcelain to the center of the table.

I exhale.

She tells me how she would crawl under Elfriede's covers every night, how Elfriede would hold her and whisper in her ear until she fell asleep. She remembers white enameled beds, lined up under the eaves of a large attic, a makeshift dormitory. She remembers the light fading slowly outside the window in the gabled wall. She remembers dozens of little girls, alone, orphaned, traumatized. All around her, children cried from thirst. Many wet their beds. The nuns "treated" bed wetters by giving them bread with salt right before sleep, to "bind the water in the body." They forbade them to drink.

Against the whimpers and weeping all around, against the dying light, my mother remembers her sister's warm body, her sister's arms around her shoulders, her sister's voice, fervent, confident, a whispered affirmation in her ear: "We won't have to stay here. We'll go back home soon."

Some little boys want to become firefighters when they grow up. Nikolai Ivanovich Vavilov, born in Moscow in 1887, wanted to end famine. His father had grown up in poverty and hunger because, over and over, Russian crops had failed. As a young scientist, Vavilov soon realized that ending famine depends on the ability of plants to resist adversity: drought and flood, heat and hail, attacks by snails and locusts, rots and molds. He read everything he could about the fledgling field of genetics, sure that it might help him to understand plant immunity. As a researcher, he traveled the world, collecting tubers and seeds.

During World War II, hunger threatened not only children, not only soldiers, but also the seed varieties that Vavilov had amassed in his Leningrad institute, sure that this genetic treasure trove would, one day, save humanity from future famines. From September of 1941 through January of 1943, Wehrmacht soldiers besieged Leningrad. Stalin had ordered the city's art to be evacuated from the museums ahead of the siege—but he provided no aid at all to save Vavilov's tubers, bulbs, and seeds. Collecting plants had been declared "bourgeois" by the communist regime—a gentleman's pastime rather than what would be needed to avert famine from ordinary people.

By the time of the siege, Vavilov himself had been arrested and was slowly starving to death in prison. The scientists left behind in his institute understood that the future food security of their people was in their hands. They also understood that they were sitting on a cornucopia of edible grain and potatoes, in the center of a city that would starve.

Vavilov's botanists armed themselves. They took turns patrolling on the roof, day and night, their guns in full display. They fought mold and rats. The rats, too, were crazed from hunger. They had multiplied because desperate people had eaten most of Leningrad's cats. Vavilov's scientists stayed and stayed, tending to the crops in their care all through the siege, without ever eating them themselves. Several of them starved to death as they were tending to the collection, surrounded by bags of wheat.

Based on what I can gather from my grandfather's letters, Anna and Elfriede must have spent about two months in the orphanage, from late August until the end of October in 1943. In the middle of this, Elfriede turned six—far from her parents. I doubt that there were presents. I doubt there was a birthday cake. Sixty nights of making sure her sister's teeth were brushed. Sixty nights of whispering affirmations in her sister's ear as children cried all around.

Eventually, I ask my mother if she will check in with Elfriede about her memories of the orphanage when she next calls.

"Elfriede says she remembers nothing," my mother reports back the next time we talk. "Except that we were there forever, and that she thought we would never get back home."

I think of five-year-old Elfriede, in an orphanage full of children labeled "Class III," desperate children, thirsty children, children who wet their beds and cried themselves to sleep. I watch Elfriede in the dining hall, tall in her shortness, her hand snapped tight around my mother's wrist: instructed by her father, in writing, not just to take care of herself without her mother, but to watch her sister, to prevent her "follies." I think of how closely "Group III" in Baden-Württemberg's 1938 *Erlass* describes, in terrible words, the many foster children that my aunt will, eventually, collect into her home.

We now know that psychoses can be triggered by childhood traumas like bullying, physical abuse, moving, and abandonment. What marks a manic episode, in part, is grandiosity: The unshakable conviction that you can accomplish *anything*. Walk on water. Heal the sick. Protect your sister. Pray your mother back to health, your father safe through gunfire and grenades, your sister and yourself onto a train back home. Mania can increase goal-directed activities and reduce the need for sleep. A review article titled "Developmental and Personality

Aspects of War and Military Violence," published in the journal *Traumatology* in 2003, identifies children between the ages of five and nine as most vulnerable to developing psychiatric illnesses after war; girls are more likely to show symptoms than boys. Maybe human physiology and genes were selected for this triggering, this trait: a switch, activated by extreme stress, that transmutes tiny girls into superwomen who pull their younger siblings through.

My mother says that, one day, the nuns in Schönebürg put her and Elfriede back on a train. She remembers that both of them were wearing cardboard signs around their necks. The signs spelled out their names and the station where the conductor was to make them get off: Schussenried.

My mother remembers seeing her father there, waiting for them, on the railroad platform: one arm protectively around her mother's shoulders, the other hand securing baby Alfred's pram. She remembers the gratitude her parents expressed for having found a room in Schussenried, in the house of a couple named Baus, how kind their new landlords were, how my grandparents trusted them so much that they asked them to serve as baby Alfred's godparents.

Herr Baus worked as a nurse in Schussenried's psychiatric hospital—the same hospital where patients behind a barred window had dangled a doll made of dirty rags toward Anna and Elfriede months before. My mother remembers hushed conversations. She remembers how Herr Baus would return from work and collapse at the kitchen table, put his head down onto his arms, and sob.

Later, Oma Lotte told my mother that Herr Baus broke down in tears, again and again, as he told her how his patients had disappeared into gray buses with painted-over windows, bound for Grafeneck. I've looked it up. Between June and November of 1940, eight "transports" conveyed an estimated six hundred patients from Schussenried to Grafeneck Castle, where they were gassed, usually on the day of their arrival. Grafeneck Castle was the place where gas chambers were first invented and perfected, before they were installed in concentration camps.

After the bus transports stopped, doctors ordered Herr Baus to inject patients with lethal medicine. He said he refused—only to be forced to watch the doctors administer the injections themselves.

Schussenried's psychiatric hospital, in operation since 1875, is still housed on the abbey's grounds, though it moved into newly constructed buildings twenty years ago. The train no longer stops at the abbey, but satellite views on Google Maps show a large parking lot: the baroque library and church remain a popular tourist destination to this day. The bars across the windows of the former hospital are no longer in evidence—buildings that used to house patients now host art and cultural exhibits, business meetings for companies, and conventions for churches and special interest groups.

When I ask my mother about Schussenried, she reminds me that we, too, were tourists there, in 1982, when we walked around the immaculate grounds on a trip with my Oma Lotte. I remember the journey, the bright-white buildings, but not my mother's shock at the missing bars across the windows, the traces of her horror cleared away. Now, over the phone, she tells me how deeply disturbed she was to find nothing to remind visitors of the people behind the bars. The dangling rag doll still haunts her dreams, the shouts from behind a barred window above her head, distorted faces, waving arms. Each time Elfriede is hospitalized, my mother just knows she's there, behind those bars. Her adult mind understands that her sister never was committed to Schussenried but to Marienborn, a different monastery hospital, in the Eiffel mountains, far to the north. And yet the doll keeps rising in her dreams. To Anna, Elfriede is here, forever here, with the shouting, waving people, the people with big mouths, big eyes, behind iron bars.

Others share my mother's pain about the erasure of the psychiatric hospital's terrible history under Nazi rule. In 1983, Schussenried's protestant minister finally succeeded in having a small plaque installed on the hospital patients' division of the local cemetery. Ten years later, the artist Verena Kraft was commissioned to erect a memorial to the "victims of euthanasia" on the monastery grounds: a sculpture of concrete pillars and a concrete doorframe, outlining a room made of air, with no walls or ceiling, to signify the utter vulnerability of psychiatric patients. Each year since the installation of the sculpture, officials and community members have held a memorial service for the former patients around this wall-less room.

By the time I stood in the wheat field of the Max Planck Institute for Plant Breeding Research, the institute had been in Köln

Vogelsang for thirty years. Before that, it was called the Erwin Baur Institute, and before that, the Kaiser Wilhelm Institute, which was then located in Müncheberg, near Berlin. Its director, Wilhelm Rudorf, joined the Nazi Party in 1937, and later the SS. By 1937, he wrote about the importance of plant breeding not only for making Germany independent from imported foods, but also, and especially, for "settling" yet-to-be invaded countries to the east and north. Vavilov's research team succeeded in preserving the tubers and seeds he had collected through the siege of Leningrad. But when German soldiers marched into Ukraine, Rudorf oversaw the theft of seeds and tubers that had been accumulated, bred, and studied by Ukrainian research institutes. He employed Richard Böhme to oversee 150 women imprisoned in Auschwitz to conduct research on rubber-producing dandelions, seeds stolen from Ukraine.

By the time our sneakers squeaked over the grassy paths separating wheat plots at Köln Vogelsang, Rudorf had been retired from the institute for about twenty years. Yes. Retired. Böhme had been clubbed to death as he fled from Russian soldiers. But Rudorf, his boss, was "denazified" by British forces, with essentially no consequence, and kept his post as director of the institute. From his position, he prevented reemployment of Jewish plant scientists who had fled Germany to save their lives.

Once, when I researched Elisabethenpflege, Schönebürg, I found posted transcripts from the orphanage's record book. The Mother Superior of the Elizabethan nuns wrote in the book that, at some point during the war, she cut out and burned all pages from 1933 onward to prevent information about newly admitted children from falling into the hands of Nazi authorities. She then tried to rewrite what she could, from memory, years later. The reconstructed entry for February 1940 explains: "The local police want to know which of our wards have criminal tendencies or parents with criminal tendencies. These children are to be listed. They fingerprinted twelve children."

The psychiatric hospital in Marienborn where Elfriede stayed was established in 1888 by Cellite nuns as permanent housing for Catholic women suffering from intellectual and psychiatric disabilities. When Hitler was elected in 1933, the sisters at Marienborn were caring for 700 women suffering from epilepsy or from psychiatric conditions like bipolar disorder or depression. From 1941 to 1943, the Gestapo "selected" 490 of these women to be bussed to the psychiatric hospital at Hadamar, where they were killed by lethal injection, medication overdose, or gas: Anyone deemed "unfit to work," and hence "a drain on the economic resources or genetic health of the *Volk*," could end up on that bus.

The use of the word "selection" by both plant breeders and the Gestapo was no accident.

Five years ago, Elfriede finally agreed to move into assisted living. She says she likes her room, her bed, the food. She has not been hospitalized once since she moved in. Often, her medications, now administered with regularity, make her sleepy, fuzzy-minded, dull. But sometimes when my mother asks to speak to her on the phone, she'll get a nurse who says

Elfriede is busy, singing with the other residents, or in the workshop, making art. Perhaps Elfriede's prayers saved her from the fires of hell. Perhaps they finally brought her to a place where she's allowed her scissors and her glue stick, where she sings.

Feuerlöschteich, n. m.

Literally: "fire-extinguishing pond." During the war, fire ponds were sometimes dug by hand, in response to wartime regulations. Other times, bomb craters were left open to collect water for fire crews. Ponds that persist postwar are often contaminated with nitrate, heavy metals, phosphorus, and toxic aromatic compounds because the Allies dumped confiscated German bullets and grenades into any open water to render them unusable. Where ponds were filled in after the war, the buried munitions still create hazardous and costly surprises during construction projects: In March of 2017, a 72-year-old Munich woman had to go to the press and then to court to force the government to help pay an astronomical bill for removal of 20,000 pounds of grenades, explosives, and toxic phosphorus discovered in her yard. When her family bought the property, sixty-seven years earlier, it had been an inconspicuous, flat green lawn.

Holes dug to put out fires during war were made to swallow unexploded ordnance.

What was meant to fill in holes left after war became unrecognizable as dangerous ground.

UNEXPLODED ORDNANCE

THE DAY MY MOTHER fishes Adolf Hitler from the pond is filled with springtime sun, an outpouring of unseasonable warmth upon the villages of Upper Swabia. Children—even those who do own shoes—run barefoot in the lengthening grass, buoyed by a rare reprieve from endless chores: After listening with grim intensity to the drone of the Wehrmachtsbericht emanating from the radio, mothers and grandparents on Otterswang's two dozen farms exchange silent glances, then send the kids to play outside.

Lotte has moved her three children here from the Baus family's house in Schussenried sometime in the summer of 1944, when two rooms opened up in a farm's small annex house. Staying in a single room with two small girls and an infant had become untenable. Ecstatic at the prospect of having a place where she can send for what remains of her furniture and other household goods from Essen, she said yes to the stipulation that, to use these rooms, she would have to work in the village's plant nursery. Soon after they move, Alfred is severely wounded and sent to a makeshift military hospital in Wolfegg Castle, just sixteen miles away. Doctors regularly remove more and more shrapnel from his shoulder and upper back, which continue to grow infected despite these interventions. During each operation, the doctors wonder whether to amputate his arm, then decide to give it one more chance. In between surgeries, whenever he's well enough to catch a ride on a hay wagon, a milk truck, or a sleigh, Alfred visits his family. By May of 1945, Alfred, Lotte, and the three children have made it through a cruel, long winter here, not home and not quite reunited, but glad to be far from cities, where bombs keep falling and people starve and freeze.

On this day in early May, the bigger children vanish in a flash. Little Anna bites her lips as she squints after them. Elfriede, too, has run off with her friends from school. Turning her back on the road down which the other children have disappeared, Anna swallows hard and wanders alone among stables and sheds. The dairy cows have not been turned out to pasture after the morning's milking; balancing on the lintel to the byre, Anna watches whiskered jaws perform their grinding waltz on last year's hay. Dark eyes gaze back at her, round and patient, but she remembers the wet rasp of their long tongues as they explore backs of knees or crooks of elbows for salty sweat; she will not walk down the stable aisle.

When the cat drops down the ladder from the hayloft, his black body curling and uncurling itself into a descending triplet of musical notes, she turns and runs across the barnyard to the pond, sending the ducks onto the green water in a low-voiced cacophony of private chatter, their conversations no more comprehensible than those of the adults at home. Anna's eyes follow them longingly—ducklings, unlike children, are born already knowing how to swim.

As the ducks approach the middle of the pond, a flash of white hooks Anna's gaze. She lifts her hand to shade her eyes against sparkling water wrinkled by paddling feet, catches another flash, then another. Whatever is out there with them is much whiter than the ducks. Whiter than paper, Anna thinks. Whiter even than bleached laundry flapping on a line. White as the stucco angels in St. Oswald's, Otterswang's baroque village church.

Of course an angel from St. Oswald's would not be floating in the pond. But what if it is? The clarity of calcined white shines out again, stark and ethereal against the water's green.

The first step into the shallows feels cool but not icy, not threateningly cold. The next two steps wash chilly wetness over Anna's knees; she yanks her dress up with both hands. Is the angel worth ruining her clothes? Her arms and legs shudder with the memory of slaps raining down on them—Mrs. Klopp's punishment for mud stains and rips in the brittle, reused fabric of her skirts. In Biberach there was no choice: all children dove into the dirt every time planes thundered low and fast over the neighborhood. Sometimes bullets whined and thudded anyway.

But there is nothing to be afraid of here, only another flash of white as the drifting object bobs in the wake of the ducks. Anna takes another step, then another. She pulls her hemline up to shoulder height as frigid water circles from her belly button to her back. Bunching fabric in one fist and stretching it high above her head, she steps again, her toes in search of purchase in the mud. She reaches with her other hand, inches the floating thing toward her with her fingertips.

Wading ashore, she squeezes the object tight against her chest as she stumbles back to the farm's tiny annex house. She needs to take her catch home, right now, to show it to Mother, because Mother loves beautiful things. Often—too often—she brings home flowers from the plant nursery down the road where she works. Anna has to bite down anger on those nights; delight in arranging lupines, larkspur, or bobbing globes of peonies makes Mother forget that the nursery owner once again showed his appreciation for Lotte's work by handing her flowers from an overflowing bed instead of giving her some food.

When Grandpa Wilhelm comes to visit from faraway Essen, he spends his days in Swabia wandering from one village to the next, and each night when he walks back to Otterswang, his knapsack—emptied of cigarettes, extra sheets, and small items the family can do without—bulges with potatoes, bread, and eggs. But for Mother, it is flowers, only flowers. And you can't eat them; not even the sweet-smelling peonies, not even the lupines that turn to pods like peas after their petals drop. The white thing, Anna knows, will make Mother exclaim with delight. It must be better even than the whitest rose, because the rose, after a few days, will die. Angels last: they hang in churches, fly through Mother's stories. Maybe this one is Lilly, the little-girl-angel whose wild adventures Mother always talks about.

The stone tiles in the entrance to the annex chill Anna's naked soles. A shiver runs along her spine as, yet again, she wonders if old Mrs. Lang, their landlady in Otterswang, might be a spirit now, lurking in the dark below the stairs. The few remaining village men carried Mrs. Lang's coffin out the front door a week ago. Grandpa Wilhelm, looking after them, took off his cap with one hand and gave Anna's shoulder a squeeze with the other. Only when the procession had reached the road down to St. Oswald's, he said, "They don't know how lucky they are. Essen has no wood for coffins left. I had to sit with your grandma Sophie for five nights before I found one for her." Anna still wonders why lack of wood might make grandparents sit up at night, but somehow it means that Grandpa Wilhelm will be coming back to Otterswang, to live with them for keeps. She hopes it will be soon.

The village women have aired and scrubbed old Mrs. Lang's rooms on the first floor of the annex; soap and ammonia still tinge the whiff of mold and old potatoes wafting up the basement stairs. The wooden steps to their own two rooms on the second floor reassure Anna's toes with roughness as she climbs. Having no hand free, she nudges the door to the living room open with her shoulder, then stands, dumbstruck, in the unexpected heat.

The little potbellied stove blazes orange. The room's small windows—one above the sofa, where Grandpa Wilhelm sleeps at night, and the other by the table, where they eat when Mother cooks a meal for them instead of shooing them over to the farmhouse kitchen with the cat that insists on rubbing against Anna's legs—gape wide to dissipate the scorching air.

But Mother isn't cooking. Anna can't see what she is doing, sitting at the table, hunched over a box and several fat books.

As Anna pads toward the table, something smooth and sharp-edged sticks to the bottom of her foot. She tries to scrape it off, left sole against right shin, struggling to balance while she clenches the heavy, sodden angel against her chest.

Snippets of glossy paper blink on the floor by Mother's chair. *Rip*, go her hands, dislodging a photograph from the album. *Snip*, go the scissors, setting another clip adrift from lap to floor. Sweat worms down Anna's neck. She meant to present her catch with a flourish—*Look at what I found for you!*—but now her voice sticks in her throat. She slides the wet angel onto the table, next to her mother's books and cardboard box. The *snip-snip* of the scissors stops. The dim room dulls the angel's alabaster sheen to a sodden gypsum gray.

"Oh no." Mother's voice does not sound at all like Anna has imagined it would. All flat, without a trace of lupine-purple joy.

"It was in the pond," Anna says. She licks her lips. "It was drowning!"

"Drowning," Mother's voice repeats, with no tone at all.

Anna's eyes follow her mother's, from the table upward to an empty nail on the wall above the stove, and back down to the tabletop.

"Yes," Mother says, still tonelessly. "I suppose I should have known *he* wouldn't drown."

Color rushes across Mother's cheeks as she shakes her head. Chair legs scrape against the floorboards, then her steps fade down the stairs.

Anna now can see that the angel is just a face, shaped from plaster in an oval plate, not an entire figurine. Its nose and mustache seem familiar. Her eyes wander back to the nail on the wall. She suddenly remembers that none of the angels in St. Oswald's wear mustaches. Is that why this one has been banished from the church? Is that why Father, when he visits, in between surgeries in the military hospital, stands in silence, his arm in its plaster shoulder cast sticking out at an odd angle, and stares sternly at this angel's face?

The baby moans. Anna glances at the crib. Little Alfred's arm, naked and moist with sweat, rises and drops back down, once, twice. When footsteps creak back up the stairs, Anna turns. Her eyes find the hammer dangling from her mother's hand.

"Step back," Mother says.

Will she pound in another nail? If the angel on the table is the one that used to hang here, then maybe one nail was not enough to keep it from flying out the window and falling in the pond? Anna takes a step backwards, her eyes glued to the plaster cast.

"All the way back," Mother says. "Get on the sofa. And put your face in the pillow."

There is no give in the voice, no room for questions. It is the voice from long ago and far away, the voice that tells Anna to hold on and run as a hand yanks her from sleep and down three flights of stairs, the voice that knows the bombs are coming down. Anna's legs do what it says. The sofa's leather grabs her shins; her face prickles in the pillow's velour.

The hammer's smash is followed by the baby's wail, and then, each time the baby pauses to catch his breath, the dull *clink-a-clink* of plaster shards and paper scraps, the *swish* of broom straw over unwaxed boards. Anna's face turns from the pillow's scent of Grandpa Wilhelm toward the sofa's back to take a sip of air. Her fingers pry bangs from her damp forehead, then scrabble at the stubborn paper triangle still stuck to her left foot. She peels the snippet off and curls herself around it, her back a shield against her mother's eyes. Cradling the glossy scrap inside her hand, she tilts it into the sun that slants through the tiny window.

The scrap is part of a photograph, showing just the shoulder of a man, severed by the scissors' snip. Above the dismembered shoulder is another picture, framed and hung upon the wall. The man in the framed picture wears his hair parted severely on the right. Just like the angel. And there, under the familiar nose, is the angel's small mustache.

As Anna stares, the wailing baby draws a breath. Shards and paper skitter from the dustpan's metal. The stove door jolts her body with its clang.

This is not how my mother told the story. When I ask her if she cried when my grandmother smashed the plaster plate, she says she didn't because her mother's distress seemed so much larger than her own. When I ask what she thought Oma Lotte was so upset about, she says she didn't know it then, but now she thinks it must have been because Lotte realized how easily her daughter could have drowned.

I've never pressed Mom to imagine other possibilities or reasons why, on this day in May of 1945, her mother's initial shock did not dissolve into relief, a hug accompanied by tears. A five-year-old's memories are fragments, a kaleidoscope of moments, not a logical sequence of events in which the

Wehrmachtsbericht predicts when French troops will arrive in the villages surrounding Biberach and frightened women rush to destroy any busts or photographs that might incriminate the family.

Many details of that day—the landladies, the iron stove, the sofa, the wooden stairs, the lupines, and the cat—appeared in snippets over decades of teatime anecdotes. By everyone's accounts, my great-grandfather Wilhelm really did refuse to go to the basement for five nights so he could sit by the body of my great-grandma Sophie as she lay on the sofa in their living room in Essen and bombs fell all around.

But my mother, who until a decade or so ago could not look at any films or books that touched upon the war, never connected finding Hitler in the pond to the storm her own mother saw brewing on that sunny day. Instead of talking about soldiers or French tanks, she tells me about the dream in which she drives over the black cat: my younger nephew gets out of her car, picks up the cat, and lays it on the seat between them. She wakes up screaming as its fur touches her skin.

The scientist in me pores over census data, weather records, maps, the movements of French troops through Upper Swabia. But early childhood is coded not in words and dates but in sound and taste and touch, a hollow sinking in the belly, a quiver in the knees. And so I found the curve of five-year-old Anna's spine, the turning away from her mother to look at a picture on the leather sofa, not in my mother's telling but in the way she hung up the phone a hundred times whenever Oma Lotte began to speak about the war: "Mother, I don't have *time* for that right now."

A generation of wartime children slammed down the receiver, refused to look anywhere except ahead. A generation of parents, having brought the world to smoking rubble around everybody's ankles, smashed the busts and burned the pictures, hid *Mein Kampf* behind the linens in the closet, and never learned how to explain. Only in Oz do Munchkins dance and sing after the house has crushed the Wicked Witch. In Germany, the clang of the oven door left nothing but silence reverberating in children's ears.

The pond my mother sought with such urgency during our visit to the farm in Otterswang, on a last road trip with my grandmother over thirty years ago, was nowhere to be found: one of the Langs' children told us it had been filled in soon after the war. If anything was discovered on its muddy bottom after it was drained, Mr. Lang failed to mention what it was.

And so, like a preschooler clutching a half-dissolving necklace of sticky plastic cows and ducks and cats, here I am, seventy years after my mother pulled Adolf Hitler from the pond, holding out the story I have strung to explain why she—the woman who picked up spiders by a leg to carry them outside, who asked if she might pet the iguana at the reptile zoo—recoiled in horror when my sister and I brought her a homeless cat, and always declared that the water was too cold whenever we asked her to swim.

Langzeitzünder, n. m.

In German, *lang* is "long," *Zeit* is "time," and *zünden* means "to ignite." In English, Langzeitzünder are called "delayed-action detonators" or "time fuzes." In military terms, "fuze" is not an alternate spelling of "fuse": the fuse is a simple, cord-like igniting device, whereas a fuze is designed to start a chain of increasing heat or explosions within a bomb. There are around one hundred different types of fuzes for aircraft bombs. Bomb squad members must know them inside out.

A time fuze contains a glass ampoule filled with acetone, which is designed to break as the bomb hits the ground. The released acetone is meant to gradually, over the period of a day or two, dissolve one or more celluloid disks that hold the striker back from exploding the bomb. The idea behind the time fuze was to cause explosions after the bombing raid was over, to disrupt fire squads and rescue crews, but also to cause lasting anxiety: the sense that the world could blow up at any moment.

A bomb dropped nose-first on soft ground will enter, turn, and tunnel, mole-like, then tilt skyward before it comes to rest. Inside the Langzeitzünder at the bomb's rear end, acetone from the broken glass ampoule will puddle away from the celluloid disks it was supposed to dissolve. Thousands of bombs still sit this way, nose up, under German cities. The celluloid disks in their detonators will, over time, become brittle and disintegrate on their own. No one knows how long this will take. When they give way, the bomb explodes.

When an unexploded bomb with a time fuze is found, it must be blown up in place, no matter what it might destroy, because an anti-handling device will set off the bomb as soon as the time fuze is turned in an attempt to twist it from the bomb. The men who excavate this bomb, who diagnose what type of fuze it has, and who, once evacuations are complete, return to the bomb site, alone, who climb into the hole to install a small, remote-controlled explosive charge—they've seen their fellow bomb squad members blown apart on prior bomb removal jobs. And yet they choose to do this work. They do this work because it must be done.

TWO CAMELS

EARLY ON A SUNNY MORNING in May of 1945, a seven-year-old girl stands at the western corner of Otterswang's cobbled village square, staring, transfixed, at a group of animals and men. Some of the men are splashing naked in the village fountain. Others, half dressed, wind turbans from long sheets of cloth. Donkeys and mules graze behind the whitewashed wall surrounding the churchyard green; men bustle among them with saddles, packs, and small carts. Behind the animals and men, St. Oswald's church gleams like a rectangular wedding cake. From the square's eastern corner by the council house, two camels gaze at the girl, their legs still folded beneath them, their jaws moving impassively back and forth as they chew their cud.

It has been no more than a week since French tanks first rolled through the village under the white sheets women had hung from their upstairs windows. That evening, the village announcer walked around clanging his bell, chanting a declaration that anyone out in the streets between six p.m. and eight a.m. would be detained or shot on sight.

On this morning, after changing and nursing baby Alfred back to sleep by the makeshift cooking stove that also serves to heat their sitting room, Lotte glances into the bedroom, intending to wake her two daughters for breakfast. Only Anna's tousled head is on the pillow. Elfriede isn't in the girls' bed—or anywhere else inside the tiny house. Lotte glances one more time at her two sleeping younger children, grabs her bathrobe, and stumbles down the creaky stairs. She yanks the robe's belt into a knot, clutches the collar over her chest with her left hand, pulls the annex house's front door shut behind her, and runs. Runs through deserted village streets, in her bathrobe and slippers; runs, not knowing whether to call for her daughter or to, somehow, remain invisible. She runs along the cobbled street that leads down to the church because she knows Elfriede's dogged determination to attend morning prayers, even though no one has rung the bells for Angelus at six a.m. since the curfew has been declared.

Perhaps four decades after Oma Lotte last described to me how she found my aunt gawking at naked troops and their animals by the village fountain, I retold the story to a friend with an interest in European wartime history.

"Um," my friend said, politely, but with a wrinkled nose, "I believe there *were* French colonial troops from Northern Africa in Germany at the end of the war, so that makes sense. But camels? Why would they drag camels with them, all the way north through all of France?"

Horses, mules, donkeys—these all seem useful if you intend to hunt down scattered enemy units in the Black Forest's densely wooded mountains that hunker like a bulwark between the Rhine and Upper Swabia. Lumbering desert ships, however, not only look out of place on rain-slick woodland paths, but might also prove an outright nuisance, an impediment.

How did camels appear in front of Otterswang's baroque village church? Did my Oma Lotte really mention them, or did my childish imagination paint them into the scene to complement what she said about the troops' turbans and their flowing robes? Maybe schoolbooks or old-fashioned stories enticed my mind to augment turbans with camels. Or maybe it was church: No German nativity set is complete without the *Drei Weisen aus dem Morgenland*—the "three magi from the land of rising sun"—of whom, inevitably, one is depicted as Black and one, inevitably, leads or rides a camel.

Or perhaps the camels sprang from a popular German children's song. My sister and I learned to sing "The Auntie from Morocco" at Aunt Elfriede's house; I remember evenings spent cross-legged on her living room rug, surrounded by cousins and foster cousins, belting out refrains. "The Auntie" was a favorite—the jaunty melody banished homesickness, the text was simple enough to chime in instantly, and a group of children got to yell a counter-chorus after every verse:

> I've got an auntie from Morocco and she comes. (hipp, hopp)
> Got an auntie from Morocco and she comes. (hipp, hopp)
> Got an auntie from Morocco, got an auntie from Morocco,
> got an auntie from Morocco and she comes. (hipp, hopp)

The text is sung to the tune of "She'll be Coming 'Round the Mountain." German children most likely snatched the melody from American GIs after World War II, along with the chocolate and chewing gum the men tossed to them from atop their tanks. French and American regiments traded small towns in Upper Swabia before zones of occupation solidified; maybe the children who invented German lyrics to accompany an American melody witnessed both French and American soldiers move through their villages.

"The Auntie's" camels—two of them—appear in the second verse, shouldering the song's original six white horses out of the way:

> And she's riding on two camels when she comes. (hoppity hopp)

I can't ask my Oma Lotte if "The Auntie from Morocco" might have smuggled the camels into her village fountain scene because she is no longer alive. And Aunt Elfriede disappeared three years after she taught us the song: The police pulled over her car, jam-packed with children, on the autobahn. The children were singing hymns. Elfriede was singing hymns. Each child was holding a burning candle. The police took the children away. Elfriede took herself away. For six years, my grandmother's phone rang on random nights. At one a.m. At three a.m. At five a.m. The voice on the phone was no voice. The voice was heavy breaths. My grandmother said: "Elfriede, where are you?" She said: "Elfriede, please come home." Elfriede was breaths on the phone. She reappeared at

Düsseldorf Airport six years later, when Egyptian authorities deported her. By way of explanation, she said she had been "helping prisoners" in a Cairo jail.

Even on good days, Elfriede's childhood memories seem sketchy: When my mother asked her about their time in Otterswang, she claimed to remember nothing at all. My mother also says she herself has no memories of her sister having disappeared one morning after the tanks rolled through the village, or of Oma Lotte having to go look for her. But when I ask whether she remembers anything about the end of the war, my mother smiles and recalls fascination and surprise at stepping out the door one morning and watching camels walking down the road. She describes men wearing turbans riding the camels and more men with turbans walking alongside.

"It was the first time I ever saw someone with dark skin," my mother says. "The camels walked to the end of the village, where the parents of Elfriede's best friend, Alma, had a farm, and they stayed there for a few days."

"Do you remember how many camels there were?" I ask.

"Not many. It wasn't like a caravan or anything. Maybe two."

My mother was five in early May of 1945. Might she, too, have fantasized the camels into being—a European child's role association conjured up by Black or turbaned men? When I ask her about "The Auntie from Morocco," she says she never heard of that song. When I sing it for her, she remembers the melody, but with a different text: "Von den blauen Bergen kommen wir," "From the far blue mountains here we come," a collection of camel-free stanzas that poke fun at teachers. How did two children in the same family end up with two different sets of lyrics for one song?

My mother's descriptions of the camels' motions, their size and proximity, their riders, their destination, are all detailed, vivid. It was the first time she saw camels, and first impressions leave strong memories. But perhaps the turbaned men and donkeys simply reminded her of something she had read in *One Thousand and One Nights*. Even if she didn't know Scheherazade's tales, maybe she, too, conflated turbans with the camel-leading magi in German church nativities.

I pull up wartime maps of southern Germany. If the camels were real, they would have had to walk from the city of Karlsruhe, where French troops crossed the Rhine, all the way across the mountains of the Black Forest, and on across the Neckar River valley to reach Upper Swabia, a trip of at least one hundred miles. *Someone* besides my mother and grandmother would have seen them along the way. I comb through eyewitness accounts, some of them collected by a school project in Karlsruhe, many published in regional papers. I read village chronicles assembled by local historic societies. Dark-skinned men with turbans, usually identified as "Moroccans" regardless of their nationality, appear in accounts from all over southern Germany. They march down the streets of Freiburg and Stuttgart. They scour villages and remote farms for German soldiers that might be hiding in cellars, stables, haylofts, sheds. Some of the men drive tanks or armored vehicles, some ride horses, many walk; often they are accompanied by donkeys, mules, and flocks of sheep.

But the camels only appear in a single report: Maria Margaretha Zabel, née Frey, who was nineteen years old at the time, describes camels walking by her parents' water mill on the Wutach River. The mill, known as Die Schattenmühle, is a popular tourist destination because the Wutach Gorge is a picturesque canyon. The building also overlooks a bridge, the only place for tanks to cross the river for many miles in either direction.

Maria Zabel does not mention a date in her account, but newspaper reports describe French colonial troops arriving in the villages closest to the Schattenmühle on April 26. By the most direct route through the thinly populated mountain valleys of the Black Forest, a foot march from Karlsruhe would require around thirty-three hours of walking time. The French crossed the Rhine on April 4—plenty of time for two camels to amble to the mill from the bridge over the Rhine by April 26. And plenty of time, too, to walk another twenty-eight hours from the mill on the Wutach River to St. Oswald's church in Otterswang by May 6, the day when reports from Winterstettenstadt, only six miles to the north of Otterswang, attest to "Moroccan" regiments arriving in the village from the south.

My Aunt Elfriede taught us the third verse for "The Auntie from Morocco" like this:

> And she's shooting off two pistols when she comes. (piff poff)

"Apart from the carnage in the chicken coops, no shots were fired," a farmer from Stafflangen, about twelve miles away from

Otterswang, tells the *Schwäbische Zeitung* in an interview about the end of the war. Eyewitnesses report that chickens were shot in pretty much every village; sometimes children found their heads lined up on fence rails or on windowsills. Quotes from witnesses express outrage and surprise at the slaughter—but my grandfather's letters from the last years of the war attest that German soldiers also considered the taking of enemy fowl routine: "A crow for dinner," he wrote from somewhere on the Russian front on April 29, 1943. "It's time that we gain ground again, so that crows turn into chickens."

At three years old, the German writer Gertrud Ennulat watched French soldiers slaughter chickens in the coop across the street. Throughout her life, the chickens' terrified screams and images of red blood on white feathers kept rising in her memory, unbidden. Each time she felt her body seize in gut-wrenching fear. At sixty-six years old, she decided to write about her childhood, and asked neighbors what happened on the day French troops came through her village. Only when the neighbors hinted that things had happened to people, not just to chickens, did other memories burst into existence, vivid, sudden, and complete: Soldiers rushing into a basement full of women and children. Clothing ripped to shreds as women are pushed against walls and thrown on the ground. Guns pointed at people, shots ringing out.

"First they stole all of our fowl—chickens, geese, and ducks—and everything that wasn't nailed down in the house," Maria Zabel also says about the "Moroccans" who came through the Schattenmühle. But once the chickens were dead, the soldiers forced Maria and her mother, at gunpoint, to walk across the Wutach Bridge—to trigger any mines that might be hidden there—and then to dismantle the tank barricade that German soldiers had put across it. Barricade removed, the soldiers lifted Maria up onto a tank, right below the gun, drove off into a remote valley, locked her into a shed, and fired through the walls. Maria threw herself onto the earthen floor to evade the bullets. She later dug herself out from underneath the wooden walls with her bare hands. Then, she says, "I crawled through the bushes and shrubs, since I knew every trail and path. I finally arrived home extremely weakened. It took a very long time for me to process this act of violence."

I read her account twice, and then twice more, stalling, each time, on "act of violence": *Gewalttat*. Certainly, shooting through the walls of a shed into which you have just locked a girl constitutes an act of violence. But I am left to wonder if Maria might be referring to more than her abduction and the shots. In German, "to inflict violence upon someone"—*jemandem Gewalt antun*—is an old-fashioned euphemism for rape.

Across centuries, cultural, ethnic, religious, and political divides, sexual violence has been part of war. World War II is no exception. Historians have attempted to quantify rapes by Red Army soldiers moving into Germany from the East, and also by American and British troops. Several dissertations lament the difficulty of quantifying rapes committed by German Wehrmacht soldiers on the Eastern Front during "requisitioning," during quartering in civilian accommodations, or during outright pillaging. Sexual violence against women abducted by Germans from countries they invaded was a daily threat in German labor camps.

To my knowledge, there exists no systematic study of the rapes committed by French regiments in southern Germany. The scattered numbers I discover in village chronicles and hospital reports suggest that the percentages of women who reported rapes by French soldiers may have been similar to reports for those committed by the Red Army; they hover around 15 percent in the few communities in Swabia for which I could find both estimates of reported rape cases and population numbers. In a study conducted in Germany from 2002 to 2004, only 8 percent of women who had experienced sexual violence—one in 12.5—said that they had reported it. The number of women willing to report a rape in largely Catholic villages in 1945 is likely even lower, because sex was taboo. Some books and articles contain heartbreaking accounts of German women being shunned by neighbors and rejected by their husbands after being raped by invading troops. The German police ceased to exist after the invasion, which meant that the only agency to which women could report a rape were the occupying forces—often the perpetrators. The few existing estimates of rapes during the invasion most often come from hospitals, where the worst cases were brought for help after life-threatening abuse, and from pastors, in whom women confided because they could trust no one else.

These meager numbers, then, are staggering: A reporting rate of 15 percent, multiplied by the peacetime factor of underreporting (12.5), means that, in some places, no one got away.

Some witnesses suggest that alcohol led to mass rapes by French colonial troops: "The Moroccans pillaged the distillery in Schafhausen and then attacked anyone in Magstadt who was wearing a skirt," the Lutheran pastor in Magstadt, seventy miles northwest of Otterswang, wrote in his report. "They neither spared girls only just confirmed in the church nor the oldest women. Even the parish house, where many women had taken refuge, turned out to offer no protection."

The fourth verse of "The Auntie from Morocco" goes like this:

> We'll be popping corks from bottles when she comes. (plop plop)

Village chronicles, hospital accounts, and eyewitness reports that, near universally, label perpetrators as "Moroccan" emerged from a stew of racialized fear. German xenophobia was stoked by incessant Nazi propaganda, ratcheted up throughout the war to push German soldiers to fight until the end. Racism also ran rampant in armies on all sides. There are reports of white French commanders ordering executions and public whippings of North African soldiers who committed rapes, but none for white French soldiers. US military records also show disproportionate executions of Black soldiers, relative to whites, for rapes committed in the UK and in France.

I've asked my mother about the night of the invasion. I've asked where her father was, why Lotte and the children were in the farm's annex house alone. My mother says he was probably in the military hospital at Wolfegg Castle having another surgery in between visits. His last letter from Russia is dated July 7, 1944, which likely means that he was wounded and sent to the military hospital shortly after that. It also meshes with my mother's memories of having visited him at the castle several times.

My mother remembers my grandmother's fear on the evening after the French tanks rolled into Otterswang and that it, somehow, had to do with a decree not to lock the doors. Too many reports mention this decree to relegate it to fiction. Most likely, the order was real—a measure intended to prevent German soldiers from eluding captivity or sniping at French troops. Women interpreted it as the complicity of occupying officers with the mass rapes committed by their men.

Because of the unlocked door, my mother says, they hid Lotte under baby Alfred's crib; my mother remembers strong admonishments that they absolutely could not tell anybody where their mother was. "Moroccans" were rumored to be kind to children—handing out chocolates, sharing their rations, throwing candy from their tanks. My grandmother likely decided that having invading soldiers find three small children alone, asleep within their beds, was smart, a calculated risk to spare them from having to watch their mother being raped.

"Some of the women later banded together," my mother says, "because after the first night, they no longer felt safe sleeping alone. But by then we had the French officer downstairs."

I don't know how Lotte learned that live-in French officers often protected the women in whose houses they stayed from rampaging soldiers, but my mother remembers being told that "children's prayers go right up to Mother Mary through the clouds," and that therefore she and Elfriede were to pray for a French officer to move into their house.

"And the next morning," my mother says, "there he was, knocking on our door and politely asking if he could have the empty rooms downstairs."

Women from towns where North African regiments stayed longer term do tell other stories, stories where not all soldiers look alike. Stories of sorting the "Moroccan" soldiers into "good" and "bad," of choosing to launder uniforms and turban cloths for "good Moroccans," no matter what the neighbors said. Stories of "Moroccan" soldiers putting out fires, giving children donkey rides. Stories of turbaned men like the one in Freiburg who, in search of German soldiers, entered a house full of women, his pistol drawn—and who started beaming the moment an old lady greeted him in French. "I am so sick of war," he said. "I just want to go home to my wife and to my children." But most of all, I want to remember the story of a young "Moroccan" soldier, still a boy, who was quartered with the narrator's family for many weeks. "He never knew," the narrator says, "how much we depended on the food he brought home to share from his regiment. He told my mother she reminded him of his mom, and how homesick he was. And when he had to leave, he cried."

Which parts of my nervous system hold the fear of something that my grandmother, mother, aunt lived through? What came to me in my mother's genes, her mitochondria, or in the way my grandmother's hand might clutch my wrist? How can I tell what came to me from stories, from Nazi propaganda, or from the xenophobia in which my country bathed? How do I comb these old afflictions from the tangled knot that is my present tense? Were the men my aunt Elfriede watched in the fountain by St. Oswald's church cleaning up after too many days of walking and camping along muddy roads? Or were they splashing their heads with icy water to chase away a postbinge headache?

I can find no published account of the French entry into Otterswang. In Winterstettenstadt, six miles to the north, where Moroccan troops arrived from the direction of Otterswang on May 6 and 7, chronicler Eugen Mohr reports that "single women and girls were warned about acts of violence and were able to go to a guarded collective shelter at Mayor Müller's for the night. Other than the missing chickens, no transgressions or acts of violence have become known in the village."

Known to whom? Become known how?

When I ask my mother if anything happened in Otterswang, she says: "We knew the French were doing something bad to some of the women. But we didn't know what the bad thing was or who those women were."

How much did my aunt know that morning in May, as she stood looking at the men in the fountain? How much did any of the children know? And if they knew, how did their mothers shut them up? Young children at the time were taught to address unknown adult males as "Uncle," a habit that remained widespread when I was a child. Did mothers in southern Germany tell their children not to sing about "The Uncle from Morocco," or did the children intuitively know that, to be sung, the uncle had to turn into an aunt?

If gender-switching transformed pistol-wielding Moroccans into a harmless, bizarre "Auntie" fit for children's songs, the fifth verse of the song can be read as more ironic-reversal camouflage:

> We'll be slaughtering a piglet when she comes. (oink oink)

The piglet becomes a code allowing children not to mention the chickens while simultaneously thumbing an eye at pork-avoidant Muslim occupiers, forbidden rage disguised as merriment. Read in this way, the continued prominence of "The Auntie from Morocco" in collections of German children's songs mirrors that of "She'll be Coming 'Round the Mountain," which originated as a slave hymn about the Second Coming of Christ, with "she" being His chariot. On the song's path through Appalachia, "she" became Mother Jones, Jesus' chariot in the Rapture transformed into a supply wagon, and added stanzas about white puppies and chicken and dumplings eventually sweetened the original hymn about death and destruction into something fit to be sung by Alvin and the Chipmunks. Similar disguising stanzas—drinking Coca-Cola, baking cake, scrubbing the apartment—appear in some modern versions of "The Auntie from Morocco."

As the song passed from one child to another, when did knowing but not saying turn into singing without knowing? How did my aunt learn the song she taught to us? How could she fail to recognize the "auntie's" camels as the first camels that she saw, the same ones that stayed at her friend Alma's farm?

On the night of the invasion, seven-year-old Elfriede is put in charge of keeping her mother safe. “You have to hide me,” her mother says, “and you absolutely cannot tell anybody where I am.”

Elfriede doubts that Mother can fit under the crib’s mattress, but once they peg its support into the top holes of the corner posts, moving it and the mattress as high as it can go between the slatted rails, Elfriede can lower the support down over her. Through the slats, Mother looks like a crouched animal in a cage. With the mattress in place, Elfriede threads the oversized sheets down through the gap between the rails and the mattress support, arranging them so that there is only a tiny crack for Mother to peer through. When she lifts Alfred back into the bed, the whole arrangement no longer looks like a circus cage with a curtain. It looks like a crib, a crib with a happy baby in it.

With Mother peering through the bedsheet, Alfred tucked in above her head, they practice praying: “Dear God, please protect us through this night. Please make a French officer come live in this house.” When Mother is satisfied that they know the prayer, they sing Alfred to sleep, and then Mother says the girls must go to the bedroom and keep praying there, and to remember that Elfriede must sleep in Mother’s bed tonight, and Anna must sleep in the girls’ shared bed by herself.

Elfriede doesn’t tell Mother this won’t work, because Anna won’t know how to pray or how to fall asleep without Elfriede in her bed. She just gets into bed with Anna like every night, prays with her, and holds her until Anna falls asleep. Before crawling over into Mother’s bed, she kneels on the wooden floor for another round of the rosary. Even though this late in spring the blue walls of the room no longer glitter with ice, her sister's warmth seeps from the flannel of her shirt before she finishes the first Hail Mary. She keeps at it until she reaches the required ten—one for each knuckle—then one "O my Jesus" and one "Lord's Prayer," then ten again. Under Mother's cold covers, she wraps her feet into the hem of her nightgown, pulls the feather comforter over her head, tucks her knees into her chest, and folds her hands around her shins.

Slowly, she tenses all the muscles in her body—"Hail Mary full of grace the Lord is with thee; blessed art thou among women, and blessed is the fruit of thy womb, Jesus"—then suddenly lets go—"Holy Mary, Mother of God, pray for us sinners, now and at the hour of our death. Amen." Breathe, breathe, breathe. The pastor's sister says only real Catholics are allowed to pray to Mary. Tense. "HailMaryfullofgracetheLordis withtheeblessedthouartamongwomenandblessedisthe fruitofyourwombJesus." Breathe out. And in. "Mother ofGodprayforussinnersnowandatthehourofourdeath." Breathe. Breathe. Mother also prays to Mary. But Mother isn't really Catholic. Hold. "HailMaryfullofgrace . . . fruitofyourwombJesus." Out. "Lutheratholic," Father always jokes. "Motherofgodpray . . . hourofourdeath." Breathe. In. And hold. "HailMary . . . fruitofyourwombJesus." Will Mother go to hell because she goes to St. Oswald's? Out. "Motherofgod . . . hourofourdeath." Breathe. What happens to Lutherans who pray to Mary? Last knuckle. "O my Jesus, forgive us our sins, save us from the fires of hell, and lead all souls to Heaven, especially those who have most need of your mercy."

Nachsicht, n. f.

Forbearance. Between 1700 and 1800, usage of the German word shot up from near nothing to about eight per million, then dropped to around four per million by 1930 and to below two by 1950. Lately, it has been hovering under one. Similarly, forbearance hit its heyday from 1820 to 1840 at seven per million and then declined to below one by 1925.

How do we live in a world where forbearance—patience, leniency, refraining from enforcement of debts or rights—and *Nachsicht*—tolerance, forgiveness, kind consideration of others—no longer are in fashion?

Literally translated, *Nachsicht* means "looking after."

To forebear means to control one's feelings: to endure.

TWO BUCKETS

HOME AGAIN FOR CHRISTMAS, I've barely unpacked my bags before my mother waves a yellowed piece of paper in my face. "I have to show you this!" She's beaming—by now she trusts that I am with her on any foray into her childhood memories. I unfold the paper. Though the page is wrinkled, its one neat crease suggests that someone, long ago, took great pains to fold it exactly in half. The heading is carefully centered:

> To Anna, my Dear Granddaughter
> On the Event of Your First Holy Communion!

I smile at my mother, thank her for showing me, and sit down to smooth the paper on the glass table she has squeezed into the room as my desk. The A5 size and rhombic lineation suggest that this page was cut from a child's exercise book, the kind I used for notes and drawings in elementary school science class. I skip to the signature. I can see how Lotte's father, my Great-Grandpa Wilhelm, might have turned this page from upright to horizontal, as though to make it open like a greeting card. Black letters in elegant Sütterlin script swirl across every other narrow sideways line. I glance up at my mother, who is hovering. I want her to know I feel the exclamation point, the heft that she and her first Holy Communion carried in my great-grandfather's mind.

Until this moment, all I've known about Wilhelm are the stories. Oma Lotte's childhood memories of hearing her father, night after night, pad by her bedroom on his way to the kitchen because her mother, my Great-Grandma Sophie, wanted a fresh glass of water. Once Lotte had small children of her own, in the middle of a war, her father's stoic patience drove her up the wall. But for my mother, Opa Wilhelm was the one adult who always had time for her—the one who weathered all her mischief and frustration with imperturbable calm.

Today, like every single time she mentions him, my mother says: "Every time I got mad about homework and smashed my stylus on the slate, he climbed up the ladder to the attic in Otterswang."

"Yes," I say. "I know."

"He kept his whetting stone up there, and he'd resharpen the stylus and then climb back down."

I nod. I can see the ladder's narrow rungs, Wilhelm's slow, deliberate steps. Up, up, and up. Down, down, and down.

"Every time," my mother says. "Every time."

I don't have to remind her what my father would say right now if he were in the room with us, how he would quote Wilhelm's infamous admonishment to Lotte, repeated every time little Anna broke things in a rage: "Lotte, don't hit the child. She clearly isn't right inside her head." My father finds this so hilarious because of my great-grandfather's actual word choice for "not right inside her head": *Das Kind hat'n Schlach mit'm AB Deckel.* Literally, this means "this child got clonked on her head by the toilet lid." My father repeats this so often that I know my mother and I can both hear him in our minds right now. We smile. I turn back to the paper. My mother looks over my shoulder as I read aloud:

> Sunday will be the happiest day of your entire life, a day gifted to you by our Dear Lord in His great mercy. For then you will become a member of the Catholic Church, the largest Christian community on Earth.

It takes me a moment to grasp my great-grandfather's generosity. He was Protestant, after all, from a Protestant family. Lotte, his only daughter, married a Catholic. And yet Wilhelm's words bear no trace of disappointment, no sense of loss that his daughter and her children left his church—a decision that would have caused great strife in other German families. Here is a man, a humble factory worker, who doesn't buy into dogma, who blesses his daughter and her child to find their own path to sacred community.

Wilhelm must have written this note to Anna from the dining table in Essen-Werden's elder home. He found a place there soon after the family returned home to Essen, occupied by the British, from Otterswang, occupied by the French, where Lotte and the girls had been living by that time for two or three years.

Alfred somehow organized this trip behind the backs of the occupying troops. *Organisieren*—"to organize"—was the operative verb of the time. It meant to acquire things you were not supposed to have. The alternative to "organizing" this journey would have been to leave the family's furniture and other possessions behind for an officially sanctioned train trip back to Essen with a maximum of two suitcases per adult. The family would have lost everything they owned at a time when nothing could be bought, when most houses in Essen were in ruins, a time without money, without jobs, without a functioning economy.

Evacuee families in Upper Swabia who followed French orders for their return trips were corralled in a fenced area near the railroad stations without sanitary facilities or protection from the weather. That winter, hundreds of children and adults waited with their suitcases, sometimes for days. No one fed these families as they waited for a train that might or might not come. Nobody knew what would happen to people who dutifully showed up at these camps in response to written orders received from the French military government. No one knew whether they and their two suitcases would actually arrive back in the towns from which they had been evacuated years before.

Instead of submitting to these uncertainties, Alfred organized a secret ride in a cattle car for himself, Lotte, Lotte's father Wilhelm, eight-year-old Elfriede, six-year-old Anna, and two-and-a-half-year-old Alfred, along with another little boy, his parents, and all of the two families' possessions. Inside the train car, both people and furniture would hide behind walls of baled straw. The trip would take several days, and would include many zigzag border crossings between occupation zones—French, American, British.

There would be no possibility of washing diapers along the way. For three days before they left, my mother listened as her baby brother screamed each time he was spanked for wetting his pants. On the train, she listened as the other family's small boy was threatened and throttled by his parents, desperate to keep him quiet each time the train stopped and soldiers' voices, in English, or in French, seeped through the slats, closer, stopping as the men inspected the seal on the door, finally fading as everyone exhaled.

Often, the cattle car just sat, sometimes for hours, sometimes for a day or a night, on frost-glistening rails, and no one knew where, and no one knew if or when it would move again.

Eventually, their water ran out. My mother remembers her Grandpa Wilhelm squeezing out of the cattle car's fake-sealed sliding door at night. His plan was to find the water tank where the steam locomotives were refilled in the dark, without a flashlight, then walk back along the tracks with two full water buckets, praying to not be seen and not be shot. It would be Wilhelm lugging the two buckets, because he still had two good arms, where his son-in-law had only one. Wilhelm and Alfred must have agreed that it would be better for Anna, Elfriede, and little Alfred to lose their grandpa than to lose their dad. To this day, my mother repeats this story in rote sentences, exactly, word for word, like people do when memory has gotten stuck, like a train on icy rails, a train that never thawed or moved or changed. No water. Screaming children, hushed. Her grandpa disappearing, with two buckets, down dark tracks.

Of course this cattle car, with its occasional fire in the tiny iron stove set next to freezing children, wooden furniture, and straw, this barely warmed icebox on wheels, with its bucket into which to poop and pee, was a luxury. This little frozen girl in a train on secret tracks watches a scene on slow repeat: her grandpa squeezing, sideways, through a sliding door, his hands reaching back for two buckets. She hears her baby brother scream. She does not look up and out. She will not think about the possibility of her grandpa not coming back. She is not able yet to understand her luck to be hiding with nine humans in a cattle car, nine humans who got into the car of their own free will, who can open the door to let someone slide out, who are going zigzag, yes, but north, not east. Not to Auschwitz, not to Belzec, not to Majdanek. Where millions of humans were sent and never came back.

No soldiers opened my mother's cattle wagon. Wilhelm slid two full buckets back in through the door, climbed aboard after them. No one died. Then one night, somehow, the furniture and children were carried, in darkness, from the train. Were carried through piles of rubble, down streets that were no longer streets, to Anna's uncle's apartment, where eighteen relatives would, for months and months, camp in a single bedroom, while everyone in bombed-out Essen desperately tried to find any place with enough roof and windows left to live.

-⋘⋘ ⋙⋙-

I can see Wilhelm in the eldercare home, two years after the family arrived back in Essen: how he wipes and dries his place at the dining room table, then lays out scissors, exercise book, ink, and pen, before he sits in his chair. Maybe the exercise book, with its carefully rationed pages, belongs to him. Maybe he has a buddy who has agreed to let him have one page. He uncorks the inkwell, dips the pen's nib into the ink: *Sunday will be the happiest day of your entire life.*

Wilhelm's hand moves slowly, steadily as letters find their turns, their rhythmic ups-and-downs, right-tilted by exactly thirty-five degrees:

> May the blessing you will receive in Sunday's ceremony root itself deep inside your soul and unfold more and more. May your true faith grow with every passing year and steadily increase in strength forevermore.
>
> Signed by your Opa, who loves you.
>
> Essen-Werden, March 4, 1948

I look up from the letter and my mother tells me, again, about the day Wilhelm moved into the elder home, into a narrow room he was to share with another man. How he put his suitcase down, sat on the chair beside his bed, and she, six years old and shaken to the bone at the thought of leaving him there, scrambled up into his lap and soaked his shirt with tears. He rocked her, told her it would be alright.

And it was. The people in the home loved Wilhelm, who appointed himself the man who kept the coal furnace stoked and the potatoes dug. As soon as Alfred and Lotte moved into an apartment with two bedrooms, they brought him there, to share a room with the three children until they were grown.

And so my mother remembers Wilhelm as sitting in an armchair in the apartment's kitchen, reading the newspaper, day after day, all through her teenage years, while she and Elfriede did their best to test his patience. One afternoon, they snuck up on him and touched a burning match to his paper, just to see what he would do. He dropped the pages, stomped out the flames, sat back down, read what was left. Eventually, he started marking each page he'd read with a penciled X. Sometimes they would erase one or two, just to see if he'd read the page again. He did.

I never met my Great-Grandpa Wilhelm. All I have are my grandmother's and my mother's stories, of water glasses, newspapers, and whetting stones. And now I have this page, sliced from a child's exercise book, these letters with their steady up and down. Someone, most likely my grandmother, penciled four lists of numbers, in four different orientations, on the reverse side. "Onions," one entry says. "Bread." And "money for school." I cannot read the rest. Someone saved this note as an afterthought, after it had become scratch paper to jot down groceries and worries about money to buy them with. Another cluster of numbers, in the bottom corner, look like a child's who practiced eights versus zeros, threes, and fours. Maybe my Uncle Alfred's, who would have just started school. Whoever snatched this piece of paper from the kitchen table, whoever stuck it in a drawer instead of using it to light the stove, has my gratitude.

***Luftbildauswertung*, n. f.**

Aerial photograph interpretation. Literally: "drawing value out of a picture taken from the air."

A woman sits on a rolling chair in an office building full of metal cabinets that hold black-and-white photographs shot from US and British reconnaissance planes. Watch her page through folder after folder, several hundred pictures of what is to become a construction site, looking for just the right images, taken at just the right moment. No cloud cover. After a bomb fell, but before the next one explodes and covers up the impact crater left by the first one. Watch the technician scan the one photograph that is just right, then superimpose it onto a modern satellite image on her computer screen. Watch the woman's hand as she mouses over each impact crater, clicks to measure diameter after diameter on grainy, black-and-white images. A big crater—maybe fourteen yards across—is an exploded bomb. Click and move, click and move. Click. Click. Click. She is looking for something smaller, around two yards across: a tiny black dot with a rim of lighter pixels. Watch how she clicks her mouse again, to draw a large white circle around the point where a few black pixels are framed by a grainy white halo: the *Blindgänger*'s entry wound.

HEIDEMARIE

IN THE FIRST PHOTOGRAPH of Opa Alfred and me, I am a few weeks old, eyes scrunched shut, in a long white dress and ruffled cap, cradled in my grandmother's arms. It's my baptism, and Alfred is wearing a black suit, his dark hair combed back. His head tilts toward me; he watches my face, smiling, with interested, horn-rimmed eyes. His arms dangle by his sides. Over five million German men of Alfred's generation never returned from World War II. Of those that did come home, few learned how to bend their arms to hold a child.

Perhaps the last time my Opa Alfred had held an infant was in Essen in January of 1947, when he carried the body of his newborn daughter from St. Elizabeth's hospital to the cemetery three times. The first two times, the earth was too frozen to dig a grave. It was the middle of the Hunger Winter. Large cities, like Essen, had no coal, no bread. Several hundred thousand Germans starved to death. In Russia, between one and two million people died this way. Two years earlier, Germany had starved the countries it had occupied. After the defeat, the allies forbade Red Cross deliveries of food to Germany.

Just before this new baby girl was born and died, Alfred, Lotte, and three-year-old Alfred junior were all hospitalized. Elfriede and Anna, nine and seven years old, were parceled out to relatives. Seventy-four years later, my mother still repeats the few sentences she heard her father say about that time: *He carried her across the Engelchenfriedhof three times. The ground was frozen too hard to dig a grave. She was the most beautiful baby he had ever seen*. What I want is for someone to watch over him as he walks his youngest to her grave.

By the third time, Alfred feels her weight before he has lifted her. She is there, already, on his shoulder, before he finds shirt, pants, socks, and coat in the narrow hospital locker, pulls them on. His bleeding ulcers don't require him to stay in bed. So far, despite the crippling pain, he has refused the stomach resection the doctors say he has to have.

On the stairs down from the third-floor men's ward to the basement, he already feels her crushing his left collarbone, though he carries nothing yet. The memory embedded in his deltoid and trapezius seems all out of proportion to her tiny body's relationship with gravity. He wonders what has pulled her down to earth.

The morgue attendant glances at him, wordless, then rolls out the cart holding the tiny casket for the third time. Alfred hadn't known there were such rooms in hospitals, such metal carts with creaking wheels. He should have known. He should have looked out from his own ward's window, or from Lotte's window in the maternity ward, or from little Alfred's in children's. All would have shown the cemetery across the street.

He slides his fingers under the small box. His eyes bore through cheap pine to the face he has seen only once. She is a sleeping cherub, her cheeks smooth and translucent, not crumpled like the faces of other newborns in the ward. Decades from now he will insist she is the most beautiful baby he has ever seen. Today there is no one to say this to.

He lifts. The attendant catches his wince, the electric hitch-and-stop in a movement that should be circular. Men recognize it in each other: the fragments of shrapnel boring through flesh, irretrievable, lost beneath layers of tissue that closed around ragged craters where muscle should be smooth. Wordless, the attendant seizes the casket's corners, slides her up onto Alfred's left shoulder. Not the right. Never the right, which used to be his stronger arm.

Alfred takes his time along basement corridors, allows two breaks, one on each landing up the stairs, right hand against cement, waiting for blackness to pass behind his eyes. He should have eaten the oatmeal the nurse brought in at six. But if he had, he would by now be doubled up with pain. Better to wait for dizziness to fade.

Outside the hospital's back door, air slices into his lungs. Clouds press down like lead. Since December, each day has set record lows, a cold so severe that the earth breaks metal spades. One step down the curb to cross the narrow street, one step back up. The gate through the cemetery hedge gapes straight across from the hospital exit closest to the morgue. A bitter convenience. He doesn't feel the gravel through his boots, just hears it grind. By now, it seems habitual. He is funeral-crashing, for the third time, with permission but in the company of strangers. Babies this small are buried at the foot of other graves. The first time, and also the second time, the ground bounced the gravediggers' pickaxes back toward their faces. The only way to know if a burial will actually take place is to show up at the time announced in the newspaper. Most of the phone lines that existed before the war still lie in shreds.

On this side of the cemetery, the path is lined with pint-sized graves. *Engelchenfriedhof*, they call it—graveyard of little angels. Headstones list months, lives too short to count in years. What he carries is too tiny for a stone. This time, their family doctor said to try again. He said that Alfred's daughter will be welcome in this grave. This time, the grave belongs to the doctor's child.

Again, he wonders what to tell the priest about the baby's name. "Heidemarie," Lotte had said, before the surgery, before the nurses wheeled her gurney from the operating room straight to the bathroom, where they push patients they expect to die. Who made this the routine, this lady's room seclusion at the end? Is it a Catholic thing? A medical acknowledgment that the dying deserve a quiet place? Is it a kindness to other patients in the ward, an attempt to spare them the rasping breaths that mark the end?

The nuns who run the hospital never expected them to live: not the baby, not her mother. Death may still prove them right. Lotte is out of the bathroom today, but this has been, what, her fourth caesarean? One for baby Alfred, three years ago. One for Anna, and, before that, one for Elfriede, who has just turned nine. So: four. No. Five. The child between Anna and Alfred, the one who died inside her womb, the one they never got to name, too small to live, too large to remove in any other way. He has no memories of that surgery; by the time it happened he was on his way east in a railroad car filled with the soldiers of his regiment. Shipping out to Prussia, toward what Lotte already suspected would become the Russian Front.

One too many surgeries to survive. One too many pregnancies. When he stepped into her ward this morning, running clandestine reconnaissance in bathrobe and slippers, Lotte's face slacked somewhere between asleep and comatose. All he wanted was to stay, to sit and hold her hand, to lean his forehead on her shoulder. There was no time. He also needed to look in on little Alfred, in the children's ward. The appendectomy has left him pale and scared, but he is looking better this morning, more alert. What makes a child's appendix flare just as his father's ulcer bleeds, just as his mother is rolled into life-threatening surgery? When the boy asked for his mum, Alfred told him she needed rest, that she would be in to see him just as soon as she was well.

Snow squeals beneath his feet, the sound of temperatures far below the freezing point. The nuns told him they rushed in the priest to baptize the baby within an hour after Lotte's surgery, a habitual race against devil or death, or maybe both. Alfred wonders what the nuns imagine they have done by slapping a name onto a soul. Do they see it as a postal address on her forehead, ensuring delivery to heaven instead of hell? His stomach stabs, burns, stops his steps. He fights the urge to let the box slide from his shoulder, curl around the pain. What the hell were they thinking, disregarding a dying mother's wish to name her child? Was it that Heidemarie smells too much of *Heide*, heath: honey, sun, a summer spent in freedom, running barefoot through sand and purple blooms, skylarks singing overhead? Or did they object to "heath" sounding like "heathen"? What business is it of theirs? What right do they have to disregard a dying mother's wish?

The stabbing eases. He draws a breath, takes a step. He doesn't really mind the name they chose: Maria—Mary, like the virgin. He remembers how Lotte always scoffed at the whole virginity idea, called it the magical thinking created by a church of men. But she does pray to Mary, trusts her to know the perils of a birth. Mary knows all about carrying a child to a grave.

"Maria breit' den Mantel aus"—Mother Mary Spread Thy Cloak. They'd played the old hymn on the radio, in a filthy Russian dacha, four Christmases ago. The cockroaches. The lice. Someone had lit a candle. Alfred had imagined Mary's blue coat floating down to cover up his city, his family, his home, to hide it from the planes. By then, of course, the major damage had been done. His comrades were huddled around the radio with him, cold and homesick and grateful for an evening that brought something approaching full rations. He had been looking at his boots. It wasn't shameful to feel tears, not at Christmas, not when you were thousands of miles from where bombs were dropping toward children you had seen for one month out of every other year they'd been alive. But seeing his own sorrow multiplied on his comrades' ash-gray faces would have meant they'd all melt down. And they couldn't do it, not on a single bottle of beer per man.

Alfred still carries the photographs Lotte sent that year, the faces stenciled into his brain: Elfriede's topknot and pinched cheeks, Anna's round chin. He trips, slips, grabs the baby's casket, the weight of the body inside less than the pine encasing it, the pain in his right shoulder bright hot as his arm jerks upward for the catch. The image of who he carries now exists only in his mind. No way to get it printed. No way for Lotte to ever see. No way to know if Lotte will open her eyes again on any of them: little Alfred in his hospital crib, Anna and Elfriede stashed away with family members who don't have enough to eat themselves. The acid in his stomach burns, screams for him to put down the casket, but he can't. He will not put the casket down, will not stop walking, will not have the surgery the doctors say he has to have. What do they think he is going to do, risk bleeding out while Lotte is about to die downstairs? And leave the children where? With whom?

Alfred lay Heidemarie into the grave on this third walk to the cemetery. He never had the stomach surgery. He struggled with the pain, on and off, decade after decade, through all of my mother's childhood and adolescence, until I, too, at fourteen months old, developed gastric ulcerations. I cried for hours and hours, day after day, week after week. Lotte finally packed both of us off to Essen, to see a homeopathic doctor she had learned to trust during the war. His sugar powders, administered by my grandmother with religious fervor over the next several days, resolved the pain for both of us.

On endoscopic images of stomach walls, ulcers range from small white splotches of dead mucosal cells to deepening, widening, oozing pits, to fountains of spurting blood, life-threatening hemorrhage. A break in the protective mucosal layer allows stomach acid to eat its way through muscle and blood vessel walls—the body digesting itself. Medicine has no good answers to the question of how ulcers get passed on in families. Is it bacteria, transmitted through shared ice cream cones, a kiss? Is it genetic? No one else in my family suffers from stomach ulcers. No science explains why a homeopathic powder would heal decades-old internal wounds.

Maybe seeing his own pain on my scrunched face was what it took to put the casket down. Maybe it was seeing my living, breathing skin—a baby outside a casket.

My mother took a picture of my Opa Alfred and me around that time. My eyes are open wide toward the camera. Slender, straight-backed, he crouches beside me; his earnest gaze rests on my face. His right hand lies on his right knee, the left clutches my stroller's metal frame.

Tonfilm, n. m.

My father has a favorite joke about a movie from 1955: *Das Schweigen im Walde*, which would translate as what? "The *silenting* in the woods"? The joke is that posters proclaimed this movie to be "*ein hundert-prozentiger Tonfilm*," i.e., a film that spurted sound for one hundred percent of its duration.

Did my father make this up? He would have been seventeen—ripe for cracking teenage jokes about a suffocating postwar world. But no, the *Tonfilm* subtext on the movie poster may well have been a real and necessary clarification: there is a predecessor silent film of the same title from 1929.

The joke, then, is on the advertisers, who failed to recognize the irony.

The joke is that an entire generation was blind to its own silence.

Das Schweigen im Walde was iconic for an entire genre of postwar movies called *Heimatfilm*. *Heimat* could mean home, homeland, or native country. But the meaning of the term is so heavy, so tied to a German idea of soul, that Nora Krug's 2018 graphic memoir about unearthing her family's wartime history was titled *Heimat* in German only—the English edition appeared under the title *Belonging*. Which means that *Heimat* is about affinity for place—and that it carries connotations of the English verb "to belong": to be the property of, to be a member of, or to be rightly placed somewhere.

All *Heimatfilme* were about place: the Alps, the Lüneburg Heath, the Black Forest—sparsely populated regions where the intended audience decidedly was *not* at home. *Heimatfilme* were never about bombed-out Berlin, where Berolina Films were produced and screened. What Germans wanted after the war, after the bombings, after pamphlets and films about the concentration camps, was *Das Schweigen im Walde*: to feel at home within the "silenting" of made-up forests, mountains, heath.

WHEN JOY IS A REFLEXIVE VERB

AT THE INTERNATIONAL Women's Writing Guild Conference, Hanna, a fellow memoirist, stands five feet away from me, her arms extended wide, at shoulder height. Through the college dining hall's tall windows, sun slants across her body, her closed eyes, her upturned face and hands.

Women stream by us in groups, carrying trays piled with dirty dishes toward the conveyor belt, ready for the next round of workshops. Some cast a glance in my direction as they pass, raise an eyebrow. One or two roll their eyes.

I breathe, stand still, facing Hanna. Her eyes are closed.

Hanna had moved her chair next to mine near the end of lunch. She introduced herself, explained her British accent: She grew up in the poor quarters of London, where her parents fled after the Nazis swept their Yugoslavian village in search of Jewish families. Hanna was three years old when her pregnant mother grabbed her hand and the family ran into the woods. Trains were waiting on the tracks. The trains left empty, because people in the village knew to hide and because, eventually, inexplicably, the German soldiers left.

When Hanna asked where I am from, she rebounded a good foot.

An hour later, she stands, swaying. I don't know how she can hold out her arms that long. Every once in a while, she opens her eyes, tells me what thoughts, what memories are rising in her mind. Thoughts of relatives, aunts, uncles, grandparents who refused to flee, or fled and were caught by German soldiers who conquered the next country and the next. Sometimes tears run down her face. Sometimes I feel tears trickle down mine.

Sometimes my friend, still seated at the table, asks if she should go. Each time, Hanna and I both turn to look at her, yelp: "No!"

Sometimes Hanna asks if I need to go.

Each time, I shake my head.

In his essay "Joy Is Such a Human Madness" the American poet Ross Gay claims that joy is "not a feeling, or an accomplishment: it's an entering and a joining with the terrible."

Like me, Gay draws on darkness—in his case, Rainer Maria Rilke's *Duino Elegies*.

The "First Elegy," written in 1912, reads, in retrospect, as though Rilke could foresee World War I, his conscription into the military, the ensuing depression that would silence his writing for years.

I imagine the poet's walk along the cliffs beneath Duino Castle, where he is an honored guest of Princess Marie von Thurn und Taxis. Beneath him, sun sparkles on the Adriatic's waves. He stops, breathes rosemary and salt, looks out over the expanse of blue that is the Gulf of Trieste. A voice inside him writes negations:

Denn das Schöne ist nichts	For beauty's naught
als des Schrecklichen Anfang	but terror's opening line

Joy, according to Gay, is a joining with Rilke's sense of impending terror, personified in the "First Elegy" as an angel whose embrace is insufferable, is certain death. Rilke's angel of annihilation, Gay says, turns out to be "the maker, too, of joy."

Like Rilke, Gay pictures terror as personified—as sitting, in his case, next to personified delight, on "a bridge, very high up," "their feet dangling off the side." The bridge, Gay explains, is the place where the world's children play and fall.

Schrecklich, Rilke's adjective to describe the "terrible angels" whom Ross Gay calls "the makers, too, of joy," is derived from *Schreck*. Its proto-Indo-Germanic origin, **skreg-*, describes a jump: a bang of terror that short-circuits in the brain stem and fires action potentials into muscle before thought.

Schreck is the nervous system's lightning that strikes before the fall—before language, culture, consciousness.

The German phrase *Der Schreck sitzt mir noch in den Gliedern*—literally: "the terror is still sitting in my limbs"—describes something more akin to English "shock" than fear—a body horror, bone-deep, that's felt as a flaccid paralysis.

Schreck names the shakiness that won't leave your legs when danger has skidded past, the hanging-on of panic in your nerves, your body's inability to stand inside the present tense.

Schreck is the limpness of a chipmunk dropped from the mouth of a cat, the aftermath of the nervous system's freeze response, an evolutionary trick that helped our species to persist.

Schreck lets us survive the angel's grasp.

Schreck, too, is a baby hanging in a weightless arc above her father's head, above his laughing eyes, his shouts of "wheee!" It is her limp terror before she squeals with joy.

Joy, born in the terror of the toss before the squeal, is unholdable, is already past before anyone can stick out a hand to break its fall.

Hanna's father made it to England alive but has been dead for years. She could not touch him while he lived. He never once tossed her above his head. All of her childhood was about survivors' guilt: her parents' demands that she cast her life in honor of those who died in the Holocaust, the grandparents, uncles, aunts, and cousins she never met.

"I would have liked to meet my grandparents," Hanna says. She closes her eyes, her arms still open wide.

"Ode to Joy" blasts from my parents' radios. I'm home in Germany again for Christmas, and as we cook, wrap gifts, and play endless rounds of Rummy Cue, choirs and orchestras fill our rooms beginning with the opening line, "*Freude schöner Götterfunken*," several times each day: "Joy, gorgeous spark of gods."

The German poet Friedrich Schiller wrote "An die Freude," the poem that became Beethoven's "Ode to Joy," when plucked from deprivation by a friend: In the summer of 1785, a sponsorship from the lawyer Christian Gottfried Körner brought material security into Schiller's life. Freedom from want—even from death—seemed, for a moment, possible.

"*Auch die Toden sollen leben!*" Schiller writes, a live-in guest at Körner's house. His curls fall over the ruffled collar of his shirt, quiver as his quill scratches across the page. The smell of roast chicken and the clink of glasses drift up the stairs as Körner's wife, Minna, directs the setting of the table for a dinner with artist friends. Here it is, *Freude*—joy—the prerevolutionary imagination's toss and float without a fall:

Auch die Toden sollen leben!	The dead shall live!
Brüder trinkt und stimmet ein,	Drink brothers, sing,
Allen Sündern soll vergeben,	All sinners shall be pardoned,
und die Hölle nicht mehr seyn.	and Hell shall cease to be.

Most of the words of "Ode to Joy" blur on my parents' radios. When I look up the full text during a lull in the festive rush, I find hundreds of YouTube videos of symphony orchestras with the text scrolling across the screen, children's choirs, a Russian musician who plays the song in pistol shots, and countless reminders that the Council of Europe adopted parts of Schiller's "An die Freude," with Beethoven's music, as a hymn to represent the European Union.

Across the low couch table, my father has fallen asleep in his armchair, his nose nearly touching the newspaper. I think of Ross Gay's joy, the sentence fragment about his mother, sleeping in a chair, "her mouth part open, the skin above her eyes exactly like mine."

In the first video on my computer screen, church bells ring as the camera sweeps across thousand-year-old Nuremberg Castle, the sometime residence of every German king, then the single tower of the Frauenkirche, which was built in place of the synagogue destroyed in the pogrom of 1349, then to the plaza beneath St. Lawrence Church. People walk back and forth. It's June 14, a Saturday. A musician has placed his cylinder hat upside down on the pavers. His left hand steadies a double bass, the right dangles the bow. His eyes, inscrutable behind black shades, point straight ahead. A girl—nine or ten?—wearing a red sweatshirt glances in his direction, reaches into her shoulder bag, pulls out a recorder. It's a Moeck soprano, the same brand that German children play in school. I can taste its bitter mouthpiece against my lips, smell breath-wet pear wood. She plays a reedy "Ode to Joy" and lowers the recorder. The bass strings answer her thin notes, she lifts the recorder again, and people stop walking. Cameras are trained on the unlikely duo. A cello arrives, chimes in, acquires a folding chair. Bassoons join. Violas. Oboes, violins, kettledrums. Trumpets blast—and people burst into song.

Their singing raises goosebumps on my arms. I wish I could join them. But my hesitation is not about where I happen to be sitting at this moment, across from my father, who is still asleep. The unfulfilled wish is a kind of grief. A kind of grief because I have lost my ability to sing in groups. To sing like the people in this video: swept into the moment, full-throated, loud, feet on the ground, joy twirling to the sky. When did this happen? When did I start standing by, watching, silent, tense?

I quit the school chorus when I was thirteen. I told myself I'd rather spend my time outside. But I didn't just quit chorus practice: those sessions were the last time I remember letting my voice melt into the singing of a crowd.

Around that age, German girls tend to pass around a *Poesiealbum*: a small, cloth-bound, square book in which you ask your relatives, friends, and teachers to fill a page with an aphorism, or a poem, or a small drawing they think might help you along your way as you move through puberty and into adulthood.

My music teacher, predictably, wrote a widely cited German aphorism in mine:

Wo man singt, da laß Dich ruhig nieder.	Where people sing, go make yourself at home.
Böse Menschen kennen keine Lieder.	For evil humans know no song.

When I look for its origin, I find that it was likely cribbed from two verses of Johann Gottfried Seume's poem "Die Gesänge," "The Songs," published in 1804:

Wo man singet, laß dich ruhig nieder,	Where people sing, go make yourself at home
Ohne Furcht, was man im Lande glaubt;	without fear of what folks in that country may believe;
Wo man singet, wird kein Mensch beraubt:	where people sing, no person is a thief:
Bösewichter haben keine Lieder.	for villains have no songs.

The third line makes sense, because Seume spent most of the year 1801 walking all over Europe, where roadside robbery was a frequent threat to the lone hiker. But the second line hits hard. Seume seems to speak directly of what I lost sometime in my early teens: the ability to sing without fear of what people in my country may believe. The fear is there, always there. Where people sing in groups, it balloons, grows large enough to block the sun.

But my ballooning fear is not about the single "villain," the *Bösewicht* Seume had in mind: the robber or swindler a hiker might encounter on her trip. My fear of shared singing, my inability to trust, to lose myself in song, is about the aphorism's modernized words: *böse Menschen*—evil people. The brown mass of SA men I watched singing Nazi songs as they march down the streets in school videos and in movies about the Third Reich. It's about any singers of "*Deutschland, Deutschland über alles*," that original—now forbidden—first stanza of Germany's national anthem, still, or again, belted out by German nationalists, with gusto, after beers.

I'm not sure what grade I was in when I understood that Nazis sang. That they used music to press on people's happy hormone switches in the brain to get them to forget their hardships, to stop thinking, to stop questioning right and wrong, to fall in line. We now call the state induced by communal singing "social flow," a phenomenon, likely mediated through the hormone oxytocin, in which individual identity is merged with a group and members of that group feel elated and invincible.

I still *can* sing, and I do: in the shower. When I vacuum. Or in the car, alone with my dog. With my friends' children, under the Christmas tree. But in large groups, church services, weddings, or graduations, I stand silent. Singing feels dangerous, too close to blinding ecstasy. Someone had better stay awake, keep watch. What are we singing really? Am I sure I want to go along? Is there something in this melody, behind this text, inside this feeling, that should make me scream, or maybe run?

I pull up the Nuremberg flash mob video again on New Year's Eve. I am, yet again, playing round after round of Rummy Cue with my parents, awaiting midnight. When my father takes a very long time to ponder his next move, I hit "play" and push my phone over to my mother.

"Where is that?" she asks as the camera sweeps.

"Nuremberg," I say.

"Oh," says my father, his tile suspended in midplay, "I was there once, with my youth group, after the war. I remember the plaza; everything was bombed out, just burnt rubble everywhere."

What I was taught about Nuremberg: From November 1945 to October 1946, the International Military Tribunal convened in the bombed-out city to convict twenty-one Nazi leaders and six Nazi organizations of crimes of war and crimes against humanity, including the Holocaust. Nuremberg was chosen for the trials because that's where the Nazi Party had announced the race laws in 1935: Only people who were German "by blood" could be citizens, and marital or sexual relations between Germans and people not German "by blood" (i.e., Jewish people, Roma, and Black people) were forbidden. Everything that followed, the systematic slaughter of millions of Jewish men, women, and children, was based on these laws.

My mother stops watching after the little girl plays her recorder. "Cute," she says, puts down the phone, and draws a tile. "It's your turn."

My mother doesn't just want me to get going with the game. She's trying to cut off my father's launch into retelling stories from his youth. His word-for-word repetitions make her itchy; if he won't stop, she'll leave the room.

I lay my phone face down on the tablecloth my mother knitted forty years ago. Size one yarn, the softest pastel green. Eighty thousand stitches to keep herself from jumping up from the sofa, from giving in to a nervousness that keeps her moving, moving, moving all day long.

I draw a tile and watch my father's fingers push numbered tiles across his rack in search of pattern, sequence, something he might play. I think of the pictures I saw of him with his youth group after the war, on his bicycle, in lederhosen, camping, hiking, smiling wide. Of his never-changing descriptions of climbing over rubble, playing hide-and-seek.

I think of Bessel Van der Kolk's claim that traumatic memory puts stories on repeat—that their telling never changes, unlike that of ordinary memories. I think of Resmaa Menakem's assertion that onlookers of violence dissociate from their memories, that their experiences travel across generations not just in words, but in bodies.

"Germany's grandchildren assume the critical task of mediating the past from the parental and grandparental generations to the generations following," Caroline Schaumann writes in *Memory Matters: Generational Responses to Germany's Nazi Past in Recent Women's Literature*. "They reinterpret it in ways distinctly different from previous generations, that is, with a post-unification perspective that includes inquiries into both perpetration and victimhood in Nazi Germany and the postwar era."

She means that my generation grew up in what she calls "a memory culture": a country that regularly teaches about National Socialism and the Holocaust in schools, museums, films, and books. She means our job is not just to hear our parents' and grandparents' stories—their pain, their gaps, and their contradictions with what we might know as fact—but also to make a different art, a different set of words.

Beethoven picked up Schiller's "An die Freude" in 1824. After the French Revolution, after the reign of terror and the guillotines, after Napoleon, after democracy's death as the price of peace, he thumbs through volume two of Schiller's *Gedichte*, stops, presses keys on the piano, floats Schiller's words on melody.

Schiller, by then, is not only dead but has died unconvinced of the merit of "Ode to Joy": "Your affection for this poem," he writes in October of 1800 to his friend, Körner, "is founded in the time when it was composed. But this affection is its only merit, a merit that is personal to us, not a merit to the world at large, not to poetry as an art."

Can a poet know whether her poetry is "only" personal? Two hundred years after Schiller's misgivings about his failure to do justice to "Joy," his doubts no longer matter—it has taken off, traveled mouth-to-mouth, heart-to-heart, lifted itself, song-to-song, far beyond the poet's reach.

It's June. I'm home again. Mom and I have finished lunch at the little table on my parents' balcony. Just-planted geraniums glow in window boxes along the banister. She used to grow hanging mats of petunias, vast carpets of radiant purple and pink, but the petunias needed more water than her brittle bones should be carrying each day. The geraniums are a compromise, red exclamation points that insist on joy.

Yesterday we walked through woods, taking an hour and a half to complete one mile: my father's pace. A few years ago he started to sing songs he remembers from his youth several times each day, something my mother finds embarrassing. But yesterday, alone among tall trees, she joined him, remembering every line about mountains, about dew, about catching the sun before roosters crow in the villages below, her sweet voice mingling with blackbird warbles, chaffinch song.

Today dad is at eldercare. It's Monday, the one day each week that my sister has arranged for Mom to have a few hours to herself. It feels weird to sit at this table without my father, the game of Rummy Cue tucked away in its zipped pouch next to his seat on the wooden bench. Mom looks at me, then brushes crumbs from the pink tablecloth.

"You know how your dad always repeats the same story about his father?"

"The story about how Opa Konrad refused to join the Nazi Party?"

My father's father, Konrad, was drafted to serve in the trenches of World War I at age eighteen. He soon was sent home with what was suspected to be a lethal piece of shrapnel in his lungs but which turned out to be a wooden splinter from a shelled barn. Drafted again in World War II, Konrad nearly drowned in a Polish river. The incident incapacitated him badly enough to be sent home again, where he was then charged with sewing officers' uniforms for the remainder of the war. When he was elected head of the local tailors' guild, officials told him he had to join the Nazi Party. His fellow tailors testified during British "denazification" after the war that he had refused to join, telling Party officials that, if chairing the Guild required joining the Party, then they needed to find themselves a different chair.

"Yes, that one," my mother says. "He always retells that each time they mention Neo-Nazis or war or fascism on TV."

I nod.

Mom looks up, into my eyes. "Every time he says that, I'm sitting here thinking: Yes, and what about my father? What about him? And my heart hurts. And I shrink."

I can feel tears rising in my throat. My father's war story loops are relentless, repeating with greater and greater frequency. Any explanation about how his words affect my mother would keep slipping from his mind. There is no good way to turn his stories off, or to keep my mother from shrinking, day after day.

⋘⋙

I've magnified and scanned my Opa Alfred's lapels in every photograph that shows him in a Wehrmacht uniform: he wears no Party badge. But it was a narrow miss. Had Alfred drawn "Party membership" on the day his boss made the members of his collective draw straws to save their livelihoods, he would have joined.

I've transcribed what's left of Alfred's letters from the front: more than a hundred pages, single-spaced. The letters don't say what he did, what it meant to be a soldier, other than homesickness, hunger, driving, digging, cold. But three sentences, from 1943, shortly before he was severely wounded and sent home, haunt me: "The day before yesterday, I had to obey a sad command. Was it necessary? Well, my stomach has settled down again."

A *sad* command? After years of battles, of shooting and watching friends die beside you, a singled-out *sad* command?

In the college dining hall, Hanna opens her eyes. "I am getting something," she says.

I feel my forehead crinkle into a frown.

"I can *feel* my father," Hanna says. "So many years of therapy, and I have never been able to *feel* him before." She closes her eyes, arms still held out wide.

I want to hug Hanna but I know I can't. All I can do is skip my workshop, stand, and watch.

Johann Gottfried Seume's poem about villains and song has twenty-seven four-line stanzas. They walk the reader through what singing does for humans, why they sing. To escape from depression. To dissolve in bliss. To experience the feeling of melting into a crowd. To calm or cheer a baby. To make work go more easily. To dream in a meadow. To express love. To take up arms, lay down your life for freedom, win a war. To celebrate. To drown out fear and pain.

Midway through his poem is a stanza I know well from my hometown:

Mit dem Liede, das die
Weisen sannen,
Sitzen Greise froh vor ihrer
Thür,
Fürchten weder Bonzen
noch Vezier;
Vor dem Liede beben die
Tyrannen.

Outside their houses' doors
old men are sitting,
joyful, they sing songs
writ by the wise,
which kill all fear
of bigwigs and of
government minions;
their song shakes tyrants,
makes them quake.

I've seen these men, my grandfather's and great-grandfather's generations, their kitchen chairs moved to sunny spots outside their front doors in narrow alleys, their pipes lit. I have never heard them sing. But this power that Seume ascribes to the now-weak, the now-supposedly-harmless, the survivors of wars that they and other men helped set into motion, is what I crave. It's what I'm digging to regain: the trust that singing can be true and wise, a taking-back of joyful power to resist the tyrant, the bigwigs, the man-machine that forces humans into cruelty and war.

My search for the text of Beethoven's "Ode to Joy" turns up a newspaper report that describes how, a year and a half after the flash mob sings "An die Freude" in Nuremberg, about three hundred supporters of the AfD, a German right-wing party, gather in front of the Staatstheater in Mainz. It is one of several demonstrations the Party has organized across Germany. Many AfD supporters thrive on xenophobic, antisemitic, and neo-Nazi ideas; the event they registered that day is titled "Against the Havoc Created by Asylum."

Across the plaza from the demonstrators' stage, the windows of the Staatstheater are open wide. Inside, over a hundred theater employees sing "An die Freude"—loud enough to interrupt the AfD speeches outside. The singers take breaks, but they refuse to stop. Eventually, a police megaphone reminds them that "coarse attempts to disrupt registered demonstrations are punishable by up to three years in jail."

I imagine standing shoulder to shoulder with the theater employees facing the open, floor-length windows, filling my lungs, feeling my entire body, from the hollow sinking place beneath my sternum on up, vibrate with song as we pump out joy, float in it, feel it carry us, feel it drown out threats and fear and hate.

"*Alle Menschen werden Brüder*," the theater employees sing, drowning out the demonstration against Germany's liberal asylum laws. The theater director, who invited his employees to rehearse "An die Freude" to "test the particular acoustics of the theater's foyer," tells the press the next day that art is honor bound to respond to ideas and beliefs like those of the AfD.

"Want to go for a coffee?" Hanna asks.

I nod. Her smile lights her entire face, making a sunny island in the rush of women converging again in the conference foyer from various workshops.

Last night, Hanna read aloud to two hundred women about hanging diapers with her mother, when she herself was barely out of them. How she was harshly admonished when she failed at household tasks, at lifting water buckets, frozen diapers, weight no four-year-old should lift.

We make our way through the stream of conference attendees, find the cafeteria, the coffee, then slide onto the pleather seats of a booth across from each other. Over the next hour and a half, she tells me more about growing up in London, in a family that spoke only Yiddish and German. About a father who carried so much survivor's guilt that he was unable to love. How she could never measure up, never be good enough to earn his appreciation. How she was nicknamed "the girl who never smiles."

She tells me that she has risked losing her job to be here because her employer did not believe her when she said that coming here was essential to her health.

In German, *Freude* acts through a reflexive verb, for which there is no English equivalent.

Sich freuen is not "to rejoice," which requires fruition or ownership.

Nor is it "to enjoy"—deriving gladness *from* something or *from* someone.

Sich freuen is reflexive—something you do to yourself: *ich freue mich*—I joy myself.

It's not your father who tosses you into that arc-and-squeal. It is your soul that throws itself.

On the last morning of the conference, Hanna finds me at breakfast, tugs my sleeve. "I want you to know you are not responsible for what your relatives did," she says. "I couldn't hug you the other day, but today I can."

Like Hanna, the German grandchild, hugged or not, must joy herself. In dense fog, she finds a shovel, picks it up. Hands on handle, boot to metal shoulder, she steps on up to push the sharpened blade deep into earth. There is a moment of suspense, when the body's full weight hovers, before the soil sighs open and the blade slides in.

Stille, n. f.

Translated as "silence," but also can mean quietude, a settling into body, into time. It's not something you do, something that requires muscle tension as in the verb *stillhalten*, "to hold still." It's what you hear and feel as calm, and peace, descends.

German poets were as obsessed with *Stille* as they were with the moon. "*Es ist so still*," writes Theodor Storm in his famous poem "Abseits" ("Off the Beaten Track")—and then proceeds to tell us about what can be heard inside a silence of sunshine upon fragrant heath: beetles rustling, the hum of bees, larks circling and circling, singing as they climb, and, far in the distance, the single chime of a village church.

Inside the single *bonnng* of Storm's far-off village church lives time—which isn't still at all. Storm publishes "Abseits" in 1847, while underpaid workers starve all over Germany and politicians fail to solve their plight. Already, to the east and south of Storm's quiet heath, famished women and men are plundering and ransacking bakeries. Soldiers bloody and kill them as they beat them back. The truth is that, as Storm's bees hum and his cottager, watching them, leans on the half door of his low-slung house and drowses in the sun, revolution, just slightly elsewhere, is well on its way.

The adverb "still," in English, means just this: the lingering of a moment—and its looming end.

DISTANCE-SLEEP-TIME-PROBLEM

MATHEMATICALLY, TWO POINTS, A and B, define a line. Practically, the line will run crooked. It will follow muddy logging tracks through woods in Upper Swabia, from Otterswang to Wolfegg Castle. It will be more than eighteen miles long. Practically, Lotte will be sleeping several paces away from the line, between two logs, behind dense shrubs. Sun will probe gaps between beech and beech, but Lotte will lie in deep shadow, beneath a clump of spruce. Watched from above, the woods will swoop, a dark eyebrow between sunny fields, framed by two roads connecting Otterswang and Wolfegg. The crooked line will keep its distance from either road, wending through maple, beech, and oak, avoiding Wolpertswende, Baindt, and Begartreute.

Around the woods, the gossip will run hot. It will zigzag, jump ditches and creeks, slither through hedgerows, zing along fence lines, village to village, mouth to mouth. The gossip will say that the wounded Wehrmacht soldiers in Wolfegg Castle's makeshift military hospital did not surrender. No one knows for certain, but everyone will talk. Everyone will assume that whoever said whatever they said will have heard it from someone who knew that whoever they heard it from would know.

Lotte will have heard the gossip. She will wonder how anyone can know what happened miles away, when no one is allowed to walk or drive from anywhere to anywhere. The gossip will suggest that maybe some French soldiers said to someone that there was a fight. The gossip will not say if anyone was killed. But it will hint, speculate, elaborate. The gossip will reek of gunfire and tanks, of unwashed men on crutches fighting with weapons they do not have, of windows broken by tossed hand grenades, of blindfolded resisters lined up against a wall. It will have nothing to say about whether Alfred is alive.

It will still be morning, still May, still 1945. While Lotte sleeps, Elfriede, Anna, and baby Alfred will be awake in Otterswang. Elfriede will be six. She'll rub sleep from her eyes, ask where their mother is. Anna will look up and around, blue eyes wide, blonde hair a fuzzy mop. She will feel a lump rise in her throat where tears punch upward, upward from her chest. Opa Wilhelm will say that their mother will be back soon, maybe in three days, maybe in two. He will unpin the baby's diaper and tell the girls not to talk to anyone about their mom. Wilhelm will toss the dirty diaper into a pail and tell himself that his daughter will be back. He will wipe the baby's bottom, powder it with potato starch. He will not let himself consider other possibilities. He will shoo everyone from the little annex house across the yard, into the farmhouse kitchen, three times a day. He will pull Anna onto his lap whenever she starts to cry hysterically about the cat that winds its way through children's calves and table legs. Wilhelm will tell the farmer's family that his daughter has gone to visit relatives. The farmer will frown. He will think of French soldiers, the decree against leaving the village, checkpoints along the roads, patrols. His wife will open her mouth to ask more questions, then glance at her nine children around the table and remind herself to close her mouth. She will yell at her boys to stop pinching each other and to pass their plates for porridge. This will only occur when there are no soldiers at the table. No one, not even the smallest child, will ask questions when the French lieutenant is in the room.

In the woods, Lotte will sleep, canvas rucksack under her cheek, coat pulled over her head. Above her, blue-capped chickadees will sing fee-fee-foo. The chickadees call their mates, announce the news. The chickadees hiss like snakes when an animal climbs toward tree holes filled with eggs. Lotte will stir, then sleep again. She will by now have slept through bombing raids, in basements full of screaming children, in basements held up by shaking walls. She will have slept on jam-packed trains with her daughters stashed in the baggage net above her head. She will have been lifted through the window onto a moving train by the same two Wehrmacht soldiers who pushed her little girls in ahead of her. The train will have chugged out of Stuttgart's station just ahead of the bombing raid and Lotte, wedged upright between strangers, suitcases, and children, will have leaned her head against the window frame. The window will have vibrated with the movement of the train and rocked Lotte to sleep. She will have slept for months in a room with another evacuee and four children, in a house where no one was welcome, where she and her children were too much. She will have slept for months in hospitals on the brink of death after each of four births. She will have slept for weeks and weeks without a letter from the Eastern front, or with letters that are many weeks old when they arrive. She will have slept curled up, knees to chin, under a crib, her baby's breaths small and quiet above her head. She will sleep here in mud scent, green-leaf scent, sun scent on pine, after the nighttime hike from Otterswang into these woods, through puddles, swishing ferns, deep ruts in logging tracks. She will sleep until darkness again seeps into beech and fir, until the great horned owl calls her onward, oo-hoo, oo-hoo, onto more ink-soup trails, from worry to worry about whether to turn here or here. There will be no moon. Only ferns, moss, and mushroom smell, only beech branches moving in the wind, only a snapping twig that may or may not be a deer, only the stop-and-listen for soldiers that might be camping, waiting, watching here—or maybe here. There will be, at the end, a silent dash from woods to barn to shack, through empty lane and street, from shadow to shadow, to Wolfegg Castle. There will be Alfred. A pus-soaked bandage around his shoulder. A whispered conversation. A half dozen hard-boiled eggs slipped beneath his mattress, maybe some bread, a smoke-cured sausage, maybe some cigarettes. And an agreement to sit tight, to wait. There will be another dash back into woods and moss, owls and chickadees.

A line, however crooked, connects A to B, village to castle, sleep to sleep. Forty years after sun pierces beech branches, pushes its fingers into firs, Lotte will fall asleep everywhere. In bright-lit church. In the back seat of the car going a hundred miles per hour on the autobahn. At the card table whenever she draws a trump. When a grandchild tells a joke. When another grandchild runs into the room, beaming, with news about good grades. When the phone begins to ring. Sleeping pill bottles will roost on books beside Lotte's bed like tiny birds. She will promise herself not to take another one, not tonight. She will take, instead, a sip of water, plump the feathers in her pillow. She will read and read and will not fall asleep. And if she does, she will startle. It will be dark. Outside her window, a streetlight will shine on wet asphalt, reflect in puddles, hang like a too-full moon over a woodland path. Her heart will hammer, ready to run.

A line from A to B will lead straight to point C. Point C will be eighty years from point A, under another streetlight. Beneath it, Lotte's two granddaughters will sit in a delivery van. The van is full of mattresses. Above the van, their mother Anna's bedroom window glows orange from a reading lamp. The younger sister, at the wheel, about to drop her older sister off, is talking about her latest appearance as a "sleep expert" on TV. The older one will smile, proud of her dazzling sister, of how she charms audiences. She will ask about yesterday's episode, about the customers who travel from far away to her sister's store to seek advice on how to get a good night's sleep. She will imagine her sister at the wheel of this van, delivering mattresses and beds, so often at night, so often on crooked Swabian roads, so often through deep woods. She will tell her younger sister about a story, a paper line that runs from A to B. Inside the story, their Oma Lotte will be sleeping two steps from a woodland path. The younger sister will lean across the gearshift and take the older sister's hand. Her eyes will shine gray beneath the falling light. They will be wide as she explains why she won't read her sister's stories. She'll say that, when she does, she cannot fall asleep.

A line drawn on a sphere will run from A to B to A. Across this globe, small girls are asking when their mothers will come home. Across this globe, women are sleeping, a step or two from straight and crooked lines. We sleep in beds made by our mothers or our daughters or our sisters, trouble birds calling in branches overhead. We sleep, our heads against someone's shoulder, against a wall, against a window, on trains or cars or planes that run from A to B. We sleep, cheeks pressed to bags taut with things we carry, afraid that what we've heard is true.

ENDNOTES

As I write this, three bombs, dropped over eighty years ago by US planes and containing a total of 5,500 pounds of explosives, are being defused in Cologne. Twenty thousand inhabitants of the city center have been evacuated, including patients from one hospital and two nursing homes, children from nine schools, and travelers from fifty-eight hotels. Major rail lines are blocked. Planes must detour around the city. The busiest bridges crossing the Rhine are closed. Barges and cruise ships have stopped. Germany holds its breath.

This book is a project of truth-finding through creative nonfiction. Some names have been changed to help protect what little privacy people I love have left in this world of electronic traceability and shifting laws and alliances. Dialogue and events are rendered as I remember them, but memory is, of course, its own genre of fiction. I offer the following notes on individual pieces as traces of my efforts to find truth in story and in memory, and as a starting point for readers who may wish to embark on their own journeys of discovery.

DEFINITIONS OF GERMAN WORDS

In addition to stories posted by local and regional papers as well as short videos shared by news stations all across Germany, several documentaries and reports informed my respect for and words about the dangerous daily work of bomb removal squads in Germany. "Explosive Altlasten—Blindgänger-Bomben" (Explosive relics: Unexploded aircraft bombs), directed by Hildegard Kriwet and first aired by Westdeutscher Rundfunk Fernsehen on October 18, 2019, gives an overview of the extent of the problem, methods of removal, and how members of the bomb removal teams handle traumatic events. This film also contains interviews with bomb squad members who witnessed the explosion of a 20,000-pound bomb with a delayed-action detonator in Göttingen that killed three of their colleagues in 2010. A slideshow with diagrams of delayed-action detonators and information on risk assessment and cost of removal of bombs containing them, documented as a case study for the small city of Oranienburg, can be found at oranienburg.de/Rathaus-Service/B%C3%BCrgerinformationen/Kampfmittelsuche/.

The scene described in the essay "Brandbombe" is based on the documentary "Explosives Erbe—Kriegsbomben im Südwesten" (Explosive relics—WWII aircraft bombs in southwestern Germany), episode 59 of *Geschichte im Südwesten*, released by Südwestdeutscher Rundfunk on October 1, 2017, which follows a trainee as he works toward becoming a full-fledged member of his bomb squad team. The *Galileo* episode "Erlebnisreportage Bombenentschärfer" (Adventure reportage: Bomb squad members), first aired on April 14, 2014, follows the routine work of a bomb removal team to showcase the types of Störkörper that might hide a bomb, and the dogged, brave patience required for their detection and removal. Numbers for Blindgänger in Berlin were sourced from the article "Wie gefährlich sind die Weltkriegs-Altlasten?" in the October 29, 2019 edition of the magazine *Cicero Online*. A news report about the discovery of 20,000 pounds of munition buried in a former fire pond, described in "Feuerlöschteich," can be found in "Zehn Tonnen Munition im Garten—und eine Familie vor dem Ruin" by Stefan Mühleisen and Jakob Wetzel, published in *Süddeutsche Zeitung* on March 10, 2017. My description of the search for unexploded bombs through aerial photographs in "Luftbildauswertung" is inspired by the *Quarks* episode "Warum Blindgänger so gefährlich sind," aired on ARD in 2021.

English-language readers interested in learning more about buried munitions can find this article on bomb removal in Germany, "There Are Still Thousands of Tons of Unexploded Bombs in Germany, Left Over From World War II" by Adam Higginbotham, published in the January 2016 issue of *Smithsonian Magazine*. Jörg Friedrich's *The Fire: The Bombing of Germany 1940–1945*, translated from the German by Allison Brown (Columbia University Press, 2008), is an extensive English-language source describing the effects of bombing raids on Germany. Readers interested in a more detailed account of circumstances in southwestern Germany, including military action and persecution of disabled and Jewish people, are referred to Jill Stephenson's book *Hitler's Home Front: Württemberg under the Nazis* (Hambledon Continuum, 2006).

My explorations of words and translations have benefitted from several web resources, including *Digitales Wörterbuch der Deutschen Sprache* (dwds.de), *Linguee English-German Dictionary* (www.linguee.com/english-german), *Online Etymology Dictionary* (etymonline.com), *Oxford English Dictionary* (oed.com), and Merriam-Webster (merriam-webster.com). Wikipedia's English and German sites (en.wikipedia.org, de.wikipedia.org) provided quick entry points into many topics and inspiration for further research. Eduard Mörike's poem "Schön-Rohtraut" appears in *"Die Augen sanft und wilde": Balladen*, chosen and interpreted by Brigitte Kronauer, and published by Reclam in 2014. The full text and an English translation of the poem can be found at Lieder Net (https://www.lieder.net/lieder/get_text.html?TextId=11706). Frequency of usage of "Nachsicht" and "forbearance" are from *Digitales Wörterbuch der Deutschen Sprache* and *Online Etymology Dictionary*, respectively.

INHERITANCE

The inheritance of fear responses in mice is described in Brian G. Dias and Kerry J. Ressler's paper "Parental Olfactory Experience Influences Behavior and Neural Structure in Subsequent Generations," published in *Nature Neuroscience* 17 (January 2014): 89–96, and in Katharina Gapp et al., "Potential of Environmental Enrichment to Prevent Transgenerational Effects of Paternal Trauma," published in *Neuropsychopharmacology* 41 (October 2016): 2749–58.

In addition to German news sources (e.g., "Name und Herkunft unbekannt" by Heike Mundzeck, *Die Zeit*, no. 20, 1977; and "Internationale Adoption ist ein Produkt des Zweiten Weltkriegs," interview with Tara Zahra, published in *The European* on August 2, 2012), estimates on the number of children separated from their parents can also be found in Hester Vaizey's book *Surviving Hitler's War: Family Life in Germany, 1939–1948* (Palgrave Macmillan, 2010).

THE PRINTING PRESS

Sonya Huber's *Opa Nobody* (University of Nebraska Press, 2008) is a personalized exploration of socialist workers' lives in the Ruhr area during the years of the Nazi takeover. A brief summary of wartime events and circumstances in the Ruhr area can also be found in "Das Ruhrgebiet und der Zweite Weltkrieg" by Michael Zimmermann, published in *Feuersturm und Hungerwinter: Zeitzeugen erinnern sich an Krieg und Wiederaufbau* (loosely translated as "Firestorm and Hunger Winter: Contemporary witnesses remember war and reconstruction") (Klartext, 2007).

The article "History of Clubfoot Treatment; Part III (Twentieth Century): Back to the Future" by Philippe Herningou, published in *International Orthopedics* 41 (2017): 2407–14, describes the Ponseti method and its predecessors in detail.

The mechanisms through which lead can induce narcolepsy are described in "Environmental Toxins and Risk of Narcolepsy Among People with HLA DQB1*0602" by G. N. Ton et al., published in *Environmental Research* 110 (2010): 567–70.

WHEN WOMEN WRITE

Descriptions of the context in which Sebald wrote his *Luftkrieg und Literatur* (Hanser Verlag, 1999) lectures can be found in Stephen Brockmann's chapter "W. G. Sebald and German Wartime Suffering," in Stuart Taberner and Karina Berger, eds., *Germans as Victims in the Literary Fiction of the Berlin Republic* (Boydell & Brewer, Camden House, 2009); in Volker Hage's article "Feuer vom Himmel," published in *Der Spiegel*, no. 3 (1998); and in Hage's 2003 book *Zeugen der Zerstörung: Die Literaten und der Luftkrieg*, published by Fischer. This book also contains the 2003 interview Hage conducted with Sebald (beginning on p. 260), in which Sebald recounts the "bordello incident."

Ingeborg Bachmann's story "Jugend in einer österreichischen Stadt" was first published in *Die Zeit* on July 15, 1960, and reprinted in Bachmann's collection of short stories *Das dreißigste Jahr* (Piper,

1961). Six undated diary pages, written by eighteen-year-old Ingeborg Bachmann in early April 1945 and published under the title *Kriegstagebuch* by Suhrkamp in 2010, are the only record we have of Bachmann's experiences during the war. They describe how she only escapes being sent to Poland for military training by signing a deposition stating that she will forgo any university education to become a schoolteacher. They also mention—in passing—the death (presumably as a result of the bombings) of a family Ingeborg knew, as well as that of a beloved pet; plotting with a friend who works in a pharmacy to steal poison that they might take in case of a Russian invasion; taking cover under trees outside of town as their home city of Klagenfurth is being bombed and low-flying airplanes "shoot a little"; the complete evacuation of all houses along the street on which the family lived and only Ingeborg remains; refusing to go to the bunker, where water flows down the walls and oxygen becomes so scarce that no one is allowed to speak, and sitting, instead, in the garden during bombing raids; and being forced to supervise schoolchildren as they are expected to dig defensive trenches in an exposed field during another bombing raid. At the end, she describes finding a doll in the basement, dressing it up, and taking it to bed with her—a heartbreaking acknowledgement of the depths of the terror she experienced during the raids. Bachmann's summer stay in the US is described in "Wie Ingeborg Bachmann ohne Pass in die USA kam" by Marc Reichwein, published by *Welt* on July 11, 2021.

Published wartime diaries and collected letters by female German authors include *Der Schattenmann: Tagebuchaufzeichnungen 1938–1945* by Ruth Andreas-Friedrich (Suhrkamp, 1947); *A Woman in Berlin* by Marta Hillers, first published anonymously, in English translation, in 1954, and then in the German original as *Eine Frau in Berlin* (Helmut Kossodo, 1959); *Berliner Aufzeichnungen aus den Jahren 1942–1945* by Ursula von Kardorff (Biederstein, 1962), published in English translation by Ewan Butler as *Diary of a Nightmare: Berlin, 1942–1945* (Rupert Hart-Davis, 1965); *Tage des Überlebens: Berlin 1945* by Margret Boveri (Piper, 1968); *Gefängnistagebuch* by Luise Rinser (Zinnen, 1946), published in English translation by Michael Hulse as *Prison Journal:*

Traunstein Women's Prison, October–December 1944 (Penguin, 1990); *On the Other Side: To My Children: from Germany* by Mathilde Wolff-Mönckeberg, translated into English by Ruth Evans (Peter Owen Publishers, 1979); *Berlin Diaries, 1940–1945* by Marie Vassiltchikov (Knopf, 1987); and *Ausgebombt: Ein Hausfrauen-Kriegstagebuch, Hamburg 1943–1945* by Ilse Grassmann (Thalacker, 1993).

Susanne Vees-Gulani's book *Trauma and Guilt: Literature of Wartime Bombing in Germany* was published by De Gruyter in 2003, and Dieter Forte's novel *Der Junge mit den blutigen Schuhen* by Fischer in 2003. Forte's interview with Volker Hage and Hage's accounts of Wolf Biermann's memories and of Gert Ledig's novel *Vergeltung* can be found in Hage's *Zeugen der Zerstörung: Die Literaten und der Luftkrieg* (Fischer, 2003). Marie-Luise Fleißer's short stories "Eine ganz gewöhnliche Vorhölle," "Der Rauch," and "Die letzten Tage und die ersten" were republished in *Erzählungen* by Suhrkamp in 2001. Ingeborg Drewitz's novel *Gestern war heute: Hundert Jahre Gegenwart* was published by Claassen in 1978, Johanna Moosdorf's autobiographical novel *Jahrhundertträume* by Fischer Taschenbuch in 1989, and Marlen Haushofer's *Die Mansarde* by Claassen in 1969. The quoted passage from Haushofer can be found on pages 46–7; the translation from the German is my own.

Aichinger's novel *Die größere Hoffnung* was first published by Bermann-Fischer in 1948, and in English translation by Cornelia Schaeffer as *Herod's Children* by Atheneum in 1963. Quotes included here are translations I produced from a reprint of the novel in *Die größere Hoffnung / Meine Sprache und ich / Verschenkter Rat* (Fischer, 1986). The cited interview with Aichinger was published in *Die Zeit* on November 1, 1996.

BURN SPIRITS

Readers interested in learning about transgenerational effects of the trauma suffered by Germans during World War II are referred to Sabine Bode's book *Kriegsenkel: Die Erben der vergessenen Generation* (Klett-Cotta, 2009), and Bettina Alberti's *Seelische Trümmer* (Kösel, 2010).

RED CURRANTS

"Ich wollte nicht sterben bevor ich eine Frau geküsst habe" (I did not want to die before I had kissed a woman), an article by Anna Hájková and Birgit Bosold posted on Tagesspiegel.de on November 22, 2017, discusses studies on the treatment of lesbian women during the Nazi regime. A brief history of the persecution of gay people was also posted by Miriam Pütz under the title "Die Verfolgung von Homosexuellen im Nationalsozialismus" on MDR.de on January 27, 2023.

A description of the role of worker-funded cycling and other sports clubs in the resistance to the Nazi takeover of Germany can be found in *"Damit alle radfahrenden Arbeiter Saarabiens unserm Vereine zugeführt werden": Die Geschichte des Arbeiter-Rad- und Kraftfahrer-Bundes "Solidarität" als Verband der Arbeiter-Sport- und -Kulturbewegung an der Saar zwischen Kaiserreich und Nazi-Diktatur* by Thomas Fläschner (Stiftung Demokratie Saarland, 2017).

SYLLABUS FOR MY MOTHER

I owe the form of this essay to Brenda Miller, whose short-form memoir "We Regret to Inform You," written as a series of imaginary rejection letters and published in *The Sun* in November 2013, first turned me on to the possibilities of the "hermit crab essay," a term Miller coined with her co-author Suzanne Paola in their anthology *Tell It Slant: Writing and Shaping Creative Nonfiction* (McGraw Hill, 2003). I suspect that my idea to try the syllabus format to create my own "hermit crab" may have sprung from reading Jill Talbot's "The Professor of Longing," published in *Diagram* 13.3. What I know for sure is that, once I had given myself permission to try the syllabus form, an enormous mass of pent-up information, rage, and tenderness that I had been unable to corral into an essay for many years finally found its place on the page in no time at all.

DROPPED STITCHES

The quoted passage from Haushofer is from p. 206 of her novel *Die Mansarde*, published in the German by Claassen in Hamburg, 1969, which I translated into English for this essay.

My description of the historic treatment of ear infections that spread to the brain is based on the article "Diagnostic Challenges in Otogenic Brain Abscesses" by Lildal, Korsholm, and Ovesen, published in *Danish Medical Journal* 61, no. 6 (2014); the authors cite as their source the 1952 article "Treatment of brain abscess," published in volume 2 of the *British Medical Journal* (pp. 871–72).

Quotes by Jörg Friedrich about the bombing of Essen are from pages 257–59 of his book *The Fire: The Bombings of Germany, 1940 to 1945*, translated from the German by Allison Brown (Columbia University Press, 2006). Quotes by Erwin Krieft are from page 76 of the 2007 Klartext anthology *Feuersturm und Hungerwinter: Zeitzeugen erinnern sich an Krieg und Wiederaufbau*. The quote by Irmgard Keun is from "Brief an Herman Kesten vom 10. Oktober 1946," published in *Wenn wir alle gut wären* (Unger, 1983).

Tranquilizer use by the generation of parents living in Germany during World War II is described in "Dieser Bärenkram muss aus dem Verkehr," published in issue 35 of *Der Spiegel* in 1988. The underprescription of psychotherapy for the wartime generation of children is reported in the article "Die Generation der Kriegskinder: Kollektive Aufarbeitung notwendig" by Petra Bühring, published in *Deutsches Ärzteblatt* (April 29, 2005).

NO ONE HAS IMAGINED US

This chapter owes its title to a line from part I of Adrienne Rich's "Twenty-One Love Poems," published in *The Dream of a Common Language* (W. W. Norton, 1978), and some of its structural references to Maggie Smith's viral poem "Good Bones," first published in *Waxwing* in 2016. The quoted line from Adrienne Rich is part of the poem "The Images," published in her collection *A Wild Patience Has Taken Me This Far* (W. W. Norton, 1981).

STAR DOLLARS

A full English translation of the "Star Dollars" fairy tale, with references, can be found online (https://sites.pitt.edu/~dash/grimm153.html) as part of a collection of resources on *Grimms' Fairy Tales* compiled by D. L. Ashliman (https://sites.pitt.edu/~dash/grimm.html). Use of fairy tales in films produced during the Third Reich is described in the chapter "Märchenfilm im Dritten Reich" (Fairy tale movies in the Third Reich) by Ron Schlesinger, published in *Märchen im Medienwechsel: Zur Geschichte und Gegenwart des Märchenfilms* (Fairy tales in changing media: On the history and present of fairy tale movies), edited by U. Dettmar, C. M. Pecher, and R. Schesinger (J. B. Metzler Verlag, 2017).

Attitudes of people in southern Germany toward evacuees are described on p. 293, p. 300, and pp. 306–310 of Jill Stephenson's *Hitler's Home Front: Wurttemberg Under the Nazis* (Hambledon Continuum, 2006), which also states that "by the end of February 1944, 44,609 evacuees from Essen had been found accommodations in Württemberg [. . .] there were in addition 3,272 people from Essen living in temporary family care centers, 638 children [. . .] in children's camps, and 27,651 workers in relocated factories, together with their families who had to be housed. Beyond that, 40,487 people—whose provenance was not given—were lodging with relatives or friends." Information about Schussenried Abbey, including a visual tour of its baroque library, is accessible at https://www.kloster-schussenried.de/.

The question of whether extreme maternal stress can lead to the death of a child inside the womb is discussed in "The Association Between Psychological Stress and Miscarriage: A Systematic Review and Meta-Analysis" by Qu et al., published in *Scientific Reports* (2017): 1731. In it, the authors state that the results of their meta-analysis "support the belief that psychological stress before and during pregnancy is associated with miscarriage. A view held by some medical practitioners and around three quarters of pregnant women, but most often dismissed by doctors and other health care professionals."

PEAR SOUP

The Nazi-run "home for mothers" in Tübingen where Lotte spent the last month of her fourth pregnancy is described by Andrea Bachman in "Lernen was eine deutsche Frau ausmachte," published in *Tagblatt-Anzeiger* on May 3, 2017.

Descriptions of circumstances at Elisabethenpflege are based on notes I took in 2013 from a website containing excerpts from the orphanage's records. An entry from 1944 stated that the orphanage's peacetime occupancy was seventy, but that the nuns were working at that time beyond their strength to take care of 116 children "and several old people." The records also stated that "more and more starving and begging people are coming to the countryside." The website containing these records has since been deactivated. Events at the orphanage are rendered based on my mother's memories. Names of nuns have been changed.

The literature on connections between childhood trauma and psychoses is extensive. Examples include "Traumatic Life Events in Bipolar Disorder: Impact on BDNF Levels and Psychopathology" by Marcia Kauer-Sant'Anna et al., published in *Bipolar Disorders* 9, supplement 1 (2007): 128–35, and "The Uninvited Guest of War Enters Childhood: Developmental and Personality Aspects of War and Military Violence" by Raija-Leena Punamäki, published in *Traumatology* 8, no. 3 (2003): 181–204, and references therein. Some of the evidence that psychological disorders including bipolar disorder can positively affect lives is reviewed in "Positive Aspects of Mental Illness: A Review in Bipolar Disorder" by Juan Francisco Galvez, Sairah Tommi, and S. Nassir Ghaemi, published in the *Journal of Affective Disorders* 128 (2011): 185–90.

Histories of the euthanasia program at Schussenried and its commemoration are described in "Die Staatliche Heilanstalt Schussenried in den Jahren 1933–1945" (The state-run sanatorium Schussenried during the years 1933–1945) by Johannes May, on pp. 75–83 of *"Euthanasie"* (Euthanasia), edited by Hermann J. Pretsch (Verlag Zwiefalten, 1996). An endnote to the article "1945: Ende und Anfang im Landkreis Biberach" (Ending and beginning in Biberach

County), published in *Zeit und Heimat* (Time and home), April 8, 1985, states that more than a thousand people from Biberach county were killed by Nazis due to race, political affiliation, illness, or disability.

Numbers of patients from Marienborn who were killed at Hadamar are sourced from the Wikipedia article "Kloster Marienborn" (de.wikipedia.org/wiki/Kloster_Marienborn_(Eifel)), accessed on January 5, 2022, which cites p. 97 and following from Harry Seipolt's *Kann der Gnadentod gewährt werden: Zwangssterilisation und NS-"Euthanasie" in der Region Aachen* (Can mercy killings be granted: Forced sterilization and NS–"Euthanasia" in the region surrounding Aachen) (Alano Herodot Verlag, 1995).

Theft of Ukrainian and Russian seeds and tubers by Nazi scientists is described by Daniel Gade in "Converging Ethnobiology and Ethnobiography: Cultivated Plants, Heinz Brücher, and Nazi Ideology" in *Journal of Ethnobiology* 26, no. 1 (2006): 82–106; in "'Rasches Zupacken'—Heinz Brücher und das botanische Sammelkommando der SS nach Rußland 1943" by Uwe Hossfeld, published in *Autarkie und Ostexpansion: Pflanzenzucht und Agrarforschung im Nationalsozialismus*, edited by Susanne Heim (Wallstein Verlag, 2002); and in *Research for Autarky: The Contribution of Scientists to Nazi Rule in Germany* by Susanne Heim (Carola Sachse, 2001).

UNEXPLODED ORDNANCE

The general circumstances experienced by women evacuated to rural southern Germany, including the expectation that they engage in field work in addition to paying for their accommodation, are described on pp. 295–310 of Jill Stephenson's *Hitler's Home Front* (Hambledon Continuum, 2006); the advance of Allied troops and its effects on the population are detailed in chapter 10. Some descriptions of events in Otterswang immediately before the arrival of Allied troops can be found in "1945: Ende und Anfang im Landkreis Biberach," published in *Zeit und Heimat*, May 8, 1985. The following passage from the article, which quotes from "Heimatbuch" by Moritz Müller, helped me to imagine the degree of Lotte's anxiety in the days leading up to the invasion:

> *On April 20 1945, plant nursery owner Theobold, his people, and the German soldiers quartering with him built a tank barricade across the so-called "little stone bridge" between Otterswang and Aulendorf to prevent the advance of the occupying troops. Inhabitants of Otterswang rightly feared that this barricade would endanger their village. Based on this concern, twelve citizens of Otterswang assembled and went to the barricade to ask the German officer in charge to have the barricade removed to spare the village from being shelled. These men knew well that they could not remove the barricade themselves, because they would be put to death. When the officer heard their plea, he called his soldiers to surround the men and threatened to have them shot on the spot. In response to many pleas, he relented from this plan, but forced the men to walk to Aulendorf to face his superior officer. When the citizens from Otterswang had already reached the brewery in Aulendorf, they were called back. The women and children who had assembled at the edge of Otterswang, because they feared for the fate of their husbands and fathers, took their concern to the paymaster of the regiment, who was named Keck and was quartered with the village priest in Otterswang and now on his way to Aulendorf. He then succeeded in convincing the superior officer in Aulendorf to release the men.*

The article also lists incidents of people being shot as punishment for other acts of "disloyalty" to the Nazi regime in Biberach county. Translation from the German is my own.

The silence that stood between the generations who witnessed the war as parents and as children was brought into public view by Sabine Bode's book *Die vergessene Generation: Die Kriegskinder brechen ihr Schweigen* (The forgotten generation: The children of war break their silence) (Klett-Cotta, 2004). An English description of the book and some translated excerpts can be found online (https://www.sabine-bode-koeln.de/war-children/the-forgotten-generation/). For a discussion on how the narration of family stories changes across generations, see, for example, "Renarrations: How Pasts Change in Conversational Remembering" by Harald Welzer, published in *Memory Studies* 3, no. 1 (2010): 5–17.

TWO CAMELS

Maria Zabel's report of camels in the Wutach Gorge was published on February 8, 2010, as part of a collection of eyewitness accounts under the title "Kriegsende: Zeitzeugenberichte I" by *Badische Zeitung* (https://www.badische-zeitung.de/zeitzeugenberichte-i). The newspaper's website also provides access to an article by Elmar Weishaar titled "Brenzlige Situationen vor und nach dem Kriegsende 1945" (Dicey situations before and after the end of the war), which reports on French troops arriving in Bonndorf near the Schattenmühle on April 26, 1945, and "Ein Pole rettet den Großvater von Bauer Dobler" by Josef Erath and Hans Willbold, which describes events in Stafflangen. Reports of "Moroccan" troops arriving in Winterstettenstadt, including quotes from Eugen Mohr, are sourced from "Erinnerungen an das Kriegsende im April 1945," published in *Der Winterstettenstetter* (supplement, Spring 2005). Eyewitness reports from the region around Karlsruhe, including a map of troop movements around Baden-Württemberg, can be found in *Kriegsende 1945: Zeitzeugen der Karlsruher Region erzählen*, by Rainer Gutjahr and Reinhold Lang, published for Arbeitskreis Landeskunde/Landesgeschichte Karlsruhe (Regional Studies Working Group/Regional History of Karlsruhe) by Verlag Megaphon in 1996. Gertrud Ennulat's memories of slaughtered chickens and women being attacked in a basement are from her book *Kriegskinder: Wie die Wunden der Vergangenheit heilen* (Klett-Cotta, 2008).

Page 160 of the report *Lebenssituation, Sicherheit und Gesundheit von Frauen in Deutschland: Eine repräsentive Untersuchung zu Gewalt gegen Frauen in Deutschland*, published by Ursula Müller and Monika Schröttle on behalf of the Bundesministerium für Familie, Senioren, Frauen und Jugend (the Federal Ministry for Family Affairs, Senior Citizens, Women, and Young People) in 2005, indicates that only eight percent of women who experienced legally recognized forms of sexual violence reported any incidents to the police.

Rapes of German women by occupying American soldiers have been analyzed by J. Robert Lilly in *Taken by Force: Rape and American GIs in Europe during World War II* (Palgrave Macmillan,

2007); rapes by Russian soldiers are described in chapter two of Norman Nairmark's *The Russians in Germany: A History of the Soviet Zone of Occupation, 1945–1949* (Belknap Press, 1997). Rapes by German Wehrmacht soldiers are discussed by Birgit Beck in "Rape: The Military Trials of Sexual Crimes Committed by Soldiers in the Wehrmacht, 1939–1944," published in *Home/Front: The Military War and Gender in Twentieth Century Germany*, edited by Karen Hagemann and Stefanie Schüler-Springorum (Berg Publishers, 2002). Discrepancies in the punishment of white versus Black soldiers for rapes committed during the occupation are described in a Wikipedia article that cites *Conqueror's Road: An Eyewitness Report of Germany 1945* by Osmar White (Cambridge University Press, 2003).

The young "Moroccan" soldier who cried when he had to leave was described by Rosina Metzger in "'Galusch' weinte beim Abschied," and the story of the "Moroccan" soldier who was sick of war and wanted to get home to his family was told by Annemarie Wiegand in "Als der Marokkaner Französisch hörte, strahlte er," both published on February 8, 2010, under the title "Kriegsende: Zeitzeugenberichte I" by *Badische Zeitung* (https://www.badische-zeitung.de/zeitzeugenberichte-i).

TWO BUCKETS

The chaotic and traumatic circumstances under which German evacuees tried to return home after the end of the war are depicted in Cate Shortland's 2001 movie *Lore*, based on the eponymous novella by Rachel Seiffert. The story also focuses on the moral dislocation of teenage Lore and her younger siblings as they discover the truth about Nazi concentration camps after their Nazi parents are arrested and the children try to reach their grandparents' home on their own.

Many accounts of evacuees from the Ruhr area about their families' multiday return journeys in freight cars can be found in the 2007 Klartext anthology *Feuersturm und Hungerwinter: Zeitzeugen erinnern sich an Krieg und Wiederaufbau* (Klartext, 2007).

HEIDEMARIE

A description of the "Hunger Winter" of 1946–1947 can be found in "Zum Hunger trat der 'weiße Tod'" by Lorenz Jäger, published in the *Frankfurter Allgemeine Zeitung* (December 27, 2009) and in accounts compiled in *Feuersturm und Hungerwinter: Zeitzeugen erinnern sich an Krieg und Wiederaufbau* (Klartext, 2007).

Based on the article "Sterbekultur im Krankenhaus: Ein würdevoller Abschied" by Rainer Prönneke in *Deutsches Ärzteblatt* no. 48 (2008), the practice of pushing dying patients into hospital bathrooms persisted in Germany at least until 1980. The author speculates that it served to repress the traumatic memories of a generation that had witnessed millions of deaths during World War II.

The potential inheritance of ulcers in families is discussed in the article "Are Genetic Influences on Peptic Ulcer Dependent or Independent of Genetic Influences for *Helicobacter pylori* Infection?" by Hoda M. Malaty et al., published in *Archives of Internal Medicine* 160 (2000): 105–9.

WHEN JOY IS A REFLEXIVE VERB

Ross Gay's essay "Joy is Such a Human Madness" can be found in his *The Book of Delights* (Algonquin Books, 2019). English translations of verses from Rainer Maria Rilke's *Duino Elegies*, Schiller's "Ode to Joy," and Seume's "Die Gesänge" are my own. The flash mob video from the performance of "Ode an die Freude" by the Hans-Sachs Chor and the Philharmonie Nürnberg was posted on YouTube by Evenord-Bank in 2014 (https://youtu.be/a23945btJYw?si=D2SDfDr_r8NPh6ul). The singing of the employees of the Staatstheater Mainz is described in "Staatstheater übertönt AfD mit Beethoven—Polizei erstattet Anzeige" by Esther Widmann, published in *Süddeutsche Zeitung* on November 24, 2015.

More information about Bessel Van der Kolk's claim that traumatic memories are repeated without change can be found in "The Intrusive Past: The Flexibility of Memory and the Engraving of Trauma" by B.

A. Van der Kolk and Onno Van der Hart, published in *American Imago* 48, no. 4 (1991): 425–54. Resmaa Menakem's ideas about bystanders of violence are explained in his book *My Grandmother's Hands: Racialized Trauma and the Pathway to Mending Our Hearts and Bodies* (Central Recovery Press, 2017).

More on the hormonal basis of the "social flow" that is induced by singing can be found in "The Neurochemistry and Social Flow of Singing: Bonding and Oxytocin" by Jason R. Keeler et al., published in *Frontiers in Human Neuroscience* 9 (2015).

The quote by Caroline Schaumann is from page 224 of her book *Memory Matters: Generational Responses to Germany's Nazi Past in Recent Women's Literature* (De Gruyter, 2008). The quote from Schiller's letter to Körner was sourced from the Wikipedia entry "An die Freude" (https://de.wikipedia.org/wiki/An_die_Freude, accessed December 30, 2019), which cites Erwin Mayer's chapter "Friedrich Schiller und die Freimaurerei und seine Hymne 'an die Freude' nach Materialien aus dem Literatur-Archiv Marbach," published in *Quator Coronati* (Jahrbuch 36, Freimaurerische Forschungsgesellschaft e. V. Bayreuth, 1999); translation is my own. Verses from Seume's poem "Die Gesänge" are cited from hor.de, a collection of German poems in the public domain. Translation is my own.

DISTANCE-SLEEP-TIME PROBLEM

I owe the title and structure of this piece to years of living with someone who taught precalculus. Sometimes the solution to an emotionally overcharged writing problem can be delivered through hearing someone rant about their students' bizarre ideas about two trains meeting on a track.

On page 325 of *Hitler's Home Front: Wurttemberg Under the Nazis* (Hambledon Continuum, 2006), Jill Stephenson states that "a German garrison with plentiful equipment" remaining in Wolpertswende precipitated a battle with the invading French troops, which claimed multiple lives and induced the French soldiers to burn down three buildings to punish villagers for the resistance. Perhaps local gossip conflated the news of this battle with that of the French takeover of the military hospital in nearby Wolfegg castle.

A description of symptoms, causes, and treatments of narcolepsy, including a collection of references, can be found at https://www.sleepfoundation.org/narcolepsy.

Gratitude to Carolyn Forché, whose memoir came to haunt the last sentence of this book. If you haven't yet read *What You Have Heard Is True: A Memoir of Witness and Resistance*, I hope you will.

ACKNOWLEDGMENTS

This book would not have been possible without the Fulbright scholarship that first brought me to the United States from Germany. At the time, well over thirty years ago, my study of plant hormone responses felt too small for Senator Fulbright's vision to "increase the chance that nations will learn at last to live in peace and friendship." Writing the essays in this book finally helped me to trust that, yes, sending students from one country to another will help us to grow into the "cultural ambassadors" we might never have imagined ourselves to be.

To Grace Talusan, Jiaming Tang, and Ilan Stavans, judges for the 2023 Restless Books Prize for New Immigrant Writing: Thank you for the depth and dedication with which you read so many amazing manuscripts. I am humbled by your trust in my words. Special thanks to Ilan Stavans for encouraging me to let both the "sciency" and the lyrical voices in my writing expand. To my wonderful editor at Restless Books, Jennifer Alise Drew: Thank you for pushing my loose collection of essays toward the wholeness that makes a book. I cannot thank you enough for the intelligent patience with which you attended to both the story arc and every sentence. Gratitude also to Lydia McOscar and Paulina Ochoa-Figueroa at Restless Books and to Alex Billington and Alex Middleton of Tetragon, London, for the thousand things that must be done to help a book emerge into the world, as well as to proofreader extraordinaire Sarah Terry. Big thanks and admiration to Beth

Steidle for the creative vision and careful attention to every detail that went into the design of the cover. Much gratitude to my agent, Mariah Stovall, for steadfast support, insightful suggestions on structuring the manuscript, and for shepherding me through the publication process.

To the readers, editors, and publishers who keep literary magazines alive: Thank you for your (so often unpaid!) work and the encouragement that you provided along the way. Many of the essays in this book originally appeared, in different form and under different titles, in the following literary journals:

"Blindgänger," "Schweigen," "Übersetzung," and "Tonfilm" as part of "An English Guide to German Words" in *The Rupture*, (formerly: 'The Collagist'), issue 108, April 2020, https://www.therupturemag.com/rupture/an-english-guide-to-german-words.

"Inheritance" as "Changing Trains" in *The American Scholar*, December 2, 2019, https://theamericanscholar.org/changing-trains/.

"Red Currants" in *The Bare Life Review* 3, 2019.

"Syllabus for My Mother" in *The Normal School*, November 10, 2021, https://www.thenormalschool.com/blog/2021/11/10/catharina-coenen.

An earlier version of "Dropped Stitches" in *Chattahoochee Review*, Spring 2020.

"No One Has Imagined Us" as "Consider the Lug Nuts" in *Booth*, 7 February 2020, https://booth.butler.edu/2020/02/07/consider-the-lug-nuts/.

Portions of "Standardabweichung" as "Four Warnings Regarding Methods of Numerical Comparison" in *Threepenny Review* 167, Fall 2021.

"Unexploded Ordnance" as "Saving Adolf" in *Bird's Thumb* 6, no. 1, February 2019.

"Two Camels" in *Terrain*, May 2021, https://www.terrain.org/2021/nonfiction/two-camels/.

"Heidemarie" as "Ulcerations" in *Blackbird* 21, no. 1, Spring 2022.

Several passages now scattered across "Dropped Stitches," "Pear Soup," and "The Camels" first appeared as "On Variance" in *The Pinch* 41, no. 2, Fall 2021.

A portion of the current essay "Dropped Stitches" was also published as "Pilot Flame" in *Orange Blossom Review*, June 2020, reprinted in 2020's Best of the Net Anthology, https://bestofthenetanthology.com/nonfiction-2020/pilot-flame/.

Much gratitude to the generous writers, staff, and supporters of the two residency programs that allowed this book to grow. To Hedgebrook—its sweet, tall cedars, wood-heated cottages, and the writers, who braved travel and seclusion during a pandemic—for providing the solitude, companionship, and sustenance to write "Two Buckets" and to assemble an early draft of the full manuscript. And to Millay Arts for circling ravens, silence, wide November fields, late-night games, wall space, and poetic inspiration as I pushed through a complete revision.

To my colleagues at Allegheny College, who never once blinked as they approved a biologist to spend a sabbatical on creative work: Thank you. Your scholarly dedication to your students and to keeping the liberal arts alive is exemplary.

To the teachers who welcomed me into classes and workshops, especially Matt Ferrence, Jennifer Brice, Marj Hahne, June Gould, Judy Huge, Katie Booth, Amy Irvine, Jessica J. Lee, Nadia Owusu, Lilly Dancyger, and Pam Houston: Thank you for your feedback on drafts and for the beautiful ways in which you encourage your students. Your comments, patience, and enthusiasm propelled and inspired much of my work. Heartfelt thanks also to the instructors who offered workshops through the International Women's Writing Guild and to the tireless staff and volunteers who have kept the Guild's workshops, conferences, and online events going for more than forty years: you held me in community when I most needed sisterly support.

Big gratitude and love to all the writers and friends who hung on through well over a decade of reading drafts of my essays, especially to Vanessa Shaffer, Juanita Smart, Laura Rutland, Lisa Freedman, Elizabeth Kaye, Stephanie Krzywonos, Linshuang Lu, Deborah Burand, Alia Payne, Alexandria Brake, Naomi Racz, Sharon Wesoky, Laura Heeschen, and the members of the Erie chapter of the International Women's Writing Guild. Special thanks to Vanessa Shaffer, Laura Rutland, Mary Jane Koenig, Chris Holder, Lisa St. John, Mary Ann Ramey, and Stephanie Krzywonos, who graciously provided feedback on early versions of the full manuscript.

And, finally: My deepest love and gratitude to the friends who have made me feel at home on both sides of the Atlantic, and to my family, who sent me out into the world and kept welcoming me back. Thank you for your love, your unwavering support, your trust, and for your willingness to share your stories and your memories. You are why and how and who I am.

CATHARINA COENEN came to the United States from Germany as a Fulbright Scholar to attend graduate school. She now teaches biology at Allegheny College in Pennsylvania. Her essays have appeared in literary magazines including *The Threepenny Review, The American Scholar, The Christian Science Monitor*, and *Best of the Net*. Catharina is the recipient of the Restless Books Prize for New Immigrant Writing, the Flash Nonfiction prize awarded by *The Forge*, the *Appalachian Review*'s Denny Plattner Creative Nonfiction Prize, a Creative Nonfiction Foundation Science as Story Fellowship, and Residencies at Hedgebrook and at Millay Arts.